Erving Goffmology

WITHDRAWN

WITHDRAWN

# Key Contemporary Thinkers

## Published

## Forthcoming

# Erving Goffman
# and
# Modern Sociology

## Philip Manning

Polity Press

The right of Philip Manning to be identified as author of this work has been asserted in accordance with the Copyright, Designs and Patents Act 1988.

First published in 1992 by Polity Press in association with Blackwell Publishers

Editorial office:
Polity Press
65 Bridge Street
Cambridge CB2 1UR, UK

Marketing and production:
Blackwell Publishers
108 Cowley Road
Oxford OX4 1JF, UK

ISBN 0 7456 0852 3
ISBN 0 7456 0853 1(pbk)

A CIP catalogue record for this book is available from the British Library.

Typeset in 11 on 13 pt Times
by Best-set Typesetter Ltd., Hong Kong
Printed in Great Britain by T.J. Press (Padstow) Ltd, Padstow, Cornwall

This book is printed on acid-free paper.

# Contents

# Acknowledgments

Various people helped with the preparation of this book. I would like to thank Irving Velody and Robin Williams from the University of Durham, Mike Emmison from the University of Queensland, Jason Ditton from Glasgow University, Doug Maynard from the University of Wisconsin-Madison, David Good and Derek Gregory from Cambridge University, and Thom Feucht, Rob Kleidman, Sarah Matthews, Bill Morgan, and Dick Stephens from Cleveland State University.

I want to thank Tony Giddens for his help throughout this project. I also profited from the extensive comments of a reviewer for Stanford University Press.

Earlier versions of parts of different chapters have appeared in journals. I would like to thank the editors and anonymous referees of these journals for their comments and the editors for permission to reuse the material: "Goffman's Revisions", *Philosophy of the Social Sciences* Vol. 18, No. 1, 1988; "Resemblances", *History of the Human Sciences* Vol. 2, No. 2, 1989; "Ritual Talk", *Sociology* Vol. 23, No. 3, 1989; "Goffman's Changing Use of the Dramaturgical Metaphor", *Sociological Theory* (Jan.–Feb.), 1991.

# 1

# Introduction and Overview

## INTRODUCTION

In this book I present a brief, but comprehensive, account
of the ideas of Erving Goffman (1922–82), and show why
these ideas are central to modern sociology. The idea that
Goffman is central to sociology is mildly ironic, because he
is often remembered as an outsider, a brilliant maverick, a
one of a kind genius, a man who is "bleakly knowing"
about modern urban life. From this view, he is a dispassion-
ate observer who sees through our day-to-day performances
and self-presentations. For example, Gary Marx tells
us that "Goffman presented himself as a detached, hard-
boiled cynic, the sociologist as 1940s private eye. His was a
hip, existential, cool, personal style" (1984: 637). Although
there is truth to this view, it does have one limitation: it
plays down Goffman's commitment to the development of
sociology. His acute observations about everyday life were
not only meant to make us think again about our day-to-
day behavior; they were also part of an abstract analysis
of social interaction. For many years Goffman tried to
develop a general theory of face-to-face interaction, a theory
that could be used to interpret any social exchange, whether
it took place in a bar or a boardroom. However, despite his

enthusiasm for this general theory, he also remained extremely skeptical about the possibility of discovering such a
general theory. It is as if he were committed to finding this
theory at one moment and indifferent to it at the next.

For his supporters, it is the tension between his attempt
to develop a theory of social interaction and his doubts that
such a theory exists that makes his work so provoking. For
his critics, this tension makes Goffman inconsistent, and his
books hard to interpret. Often Goffman seems to have two
contradictory "voices": one voice tells of a general pattern
beneath different examples of ordinary behavior, while the
other emphasizes the crucial differences between examples.

Although Goffman's attempt to develop a general
theory of face-to-face interaction is fascinating in its own
right, it also raises a question. Is it possible for sociologists
to develop a general sociological theory, a theory both of
institutions and social interaction? In his introduction to
*Frame Analysis*, Goffman wrote about the limits of his own
work while supporting the ambitious projects pursued by
other sociologists:

> I make no claim to be talking about the core matters of
> sociology – social organization and social structure. . . . I am
> not addressing the structure of social life but the structure
> of experience individuals have at any moment of their social
> lives. I personally hold society to be first in every way
> and any individual's current involvements to be second.
> (1974: 13)

In the final chapter I look at one attempt to develop
a general theory of "the structure of social life" using
Goffman's ideas. This is the structuration theory developed
by Anthony Giddens. This theory thrusts Goffman to the
center of contemporary debates about the relationship
between structure and agency. In the later chapters in
this book I suggest that in order to theorize agency it is
necessary to understand the use of rules in everyday life. I
suggest that Goffman offers an incomplete account of rule-

following, and that his ideas have to be supplemented with insights from ethnomethodology. I do not see Goffman as a precursor to ethnomethodology; rather, I believe that a combination of his ideas with theirs provides an important resource for mainstream sociology. I also believe that Giddens's theory is the best available vehicle for their delivery.

There are many ways of describing Goffman: he can be seen as a one of a kind observer, a cynic, an ethnographer, a symbolic interactionist. In this book, I portray Goffman as someone with competing visions, as someone who sees both cynical manipulation and trust in social interaction, as someone who sees sociology as both cumulative science and as humanistic enquiry, as someone who sees his own work as both a loose set of acute insights and as an organized description of the basic elements face-to-face interaction.

However, this is in the future. In the rest of this chapter I play the book as a whole on fast forward, anticipating and sketching the ideas that will be considered in greater detail in subsequent chapters.

Goffman was primarily an observer of face-to-face inter-action who possessed an extraordinary ability to appreciate the subtle importance of apparently insignificant aspects of everyday conduct. Goffman made his readers aware of this almost invisible realm of social life, with the result that the banal exchanges and glances observable in any public place become a continual source of fascination. With the exception of Simmel's, his general descriptions of face-to-face interaction are unmatched.

Let me begin with a biographical preliminary. Born in Canada in 1922, Goffman obtained a BA degree in sociology and anthropology from the University of Toronto in 1945. A chance meeting with Everett Hughes persuaded him to move to Chicago for graduate work, which led to a doctoral thesis about social interaction on a small island community off the coast of Scotland. The thesis was actually written in Paris, where he was exposed to the then fashion-able doctrine of existentialism. After completing his Ph.D.

at the end of 1953, and unable to obtain a tenure track position, he worked for Edward Shils on a project concerning social stratification. During this time he wrote the first edition of *The Presentation of Self in Everyday Life*. In 1956, a grant from the National Institute of Mental Health allowed him to move to Washington, DC to study the experience of inmates at a large urban mental hospital. In 1961, Herbert Blumer invited him to join the sociology faculty at the University of California at Berkeley. After six intellectually successful years at Berkeley, he spent a transitional year as a Visiting Fellow at Harvard, before moving to the University of Pennsylvania in 1968, where he remained until his death of cancer in 1982, at the age of 60.

Throughout his writings Goffman worked to develop a vocabulary that could describe the general features of face-to-face interaction. Although this was primarily a problem of description, it also meant that he had to explain the motivations behind everyday behavior. As a result his work contains many "how" and "why" accounts. For example, he discussed both the odd behavior of people in elevators, describing the way they stare at their feet or the floor numbers above the door and the reasons why this behavior is important to others sharing the elevator. We can understand his work as a kind of map to the uncharted world of everyday life. Goffman saves us from over-familiarity, allowing us to see the complexity, stability, and importance of apparently mundane social interaction.

Curiously, we are quite unable to explain how or even why we do most of the things that we do with supreme practical ease in our daily lives. Whether walking down a street or answering a phone call, the way we perform these activities is both more intricately patterned and more important than most of us could believe possible. In our daily lives we often act on autopilot: we comply with a set of implicit instructions that govern our behavior. Social life is patterned because we often choose to follow these instructions and thereby make the world predictable. Predictability is an astonishing collective accomplishment.

Even subtle departures from such patterns can undermine our confidence that the social world is as it appears
to be. Departures are understandable if they replace the
prevailing definition of the situation with another; they are
destructive if they cannot be interpreted. One of the major
legacies of Goffman's work is that it shows us how the
fragility of day-to-day life is lent solidity and order by small
gestures and ritual offerings. Many of the details of face-
to-face encounters (which we frequently fail to notice)
reappear in his books as examples of how our trust in an
otherwise unruly environment is maintained. For example,
when a man apologizes for inadvertently stepping in front
of someone in a queue, it is easy to miss the way he touches
her elbow as he speaks; but it is this physical contact that
assures her of the sincerity of the apology.

With the help of many examples Goffman identified the
factors that underpin our confidence in the social world.
He typically convinces us of this by suggesting scenarios
in which that world suddenly becomes quite alien and
startling. For example, when we pass pedestrians in the
street, we routinely establish eye contact for a moment,
only to then look away. This gesture is a ritual courtesy
that affirms respect among strangers in a small and almost
unnoticeable way. However, to maintain that eye contact
for even an extra few seconds before looking away transforms a gesture of support into a hostile act: it becomes
a "hate stare" of the sort practiced against Blacks in
America's deep South in the 1950s (Goffman, 1963: 83).

By scratching at the surface of many of our day-to-day
routines, Goffman uncovered a machinery of social interaction. However, it would be wrong to use this metaphor to
suggest that we are just inanimate cogs; or to put the
matter in a more contemporary idiom, just hardware for
interactional programs that churn out a predictable and
generally safe social world. On the contrary, Goffman
was fascinated by our reflexive ability to manipulate these
procedures for social interaction. Even if we often choose
to live on autopilot, casually allowing the predictable

flow of social interaction to guide us through a host of encounters, we are able to switch to manual control in order to establish our autonomy. For example, we are generally unaware of how we are sitting; nevertheless, when circumstances demand (perhaps an important interview), we are able to spend a great deal of time worrying about whether we are sitting in an appropriate way. Goffman was very alert to such occasions; in his expression, he remained "lovingly empirical". He made the mundane world refreshingly new. Unlike the traditional anthropologist who broadens our horizons by expanding our knowledge of other societies, Goffman shows us the complexity of our own.

Although there are divergences and shifting points of emphasis, it is true to say that Goffman's corpus remained focused on the study of the minutiae of social life. Unlike so many great figures in the Arts and Social Sciences, such as Marx, Wittgenstein, and Heidegger, there is not a great discrepancy between Goffman's early and late work. Instead we find continued attempts to analyze everyday phenomena and a curious willingness to abandon apparently apt ideas or "tools".

Unsurprisingly, his writings have had a profound influence on most of the social sciences, but what is surprising is that the initial excitement is often short-lived. In part, this is one of the paradoxes of success: his ideas seem so well known, his books so well read, that it is redundant to comment on them. Goffman has become an overfamiliar landmark on the intellectual map of modern social science, a person who is cited everywhere but rarely discussed in detail. Nearly all social scientists can say something about "total institutions" and the "art of impression management" but few are able to give a comprehensive account of his ideas. At best, social scientists discuss the fragment of his work that bears substantively on their own interests. This may explain why there is no "Goffman School" to continue his work.

## A SUMMARY OF GOFFMAN'S IDEAS

In his Master's thesis at Chicago, submitted in 1949, there is a protracted and ultimately vain attempt to use statistics to understand an audience's responses to a then popular American radio soap opera called "Big Sister". This work is quite unlike his later studies: it is dry, almost unauthored, and his only statistically based project. A couple of years later, in a study for the American Petroleum Institute, he studied the aspirations and frustrations of service-station dealers (people who either owned or leased petrol stations). For this, he used both quantitative and qualitative data, thereby bridging his earlier methodology with his developing interest in ethnography.

Prior to his dissertation, Goffman also published two papers, the first concerning the ways in which status symbols can be "borrowed" by those without the means to obtain them legitimately, the second about the extent to which everyday life is experienced as a huge confidence trick, in which we are all "marks" needing to be "cooled out". These two papers are a drastic departure from the quantitative approach of his Master's thesis, and the first signs of his distinctive writing style.

For his dissertation, which he was awarded at the end of 1953, Goffman spent eighteen months on a small island off the Scottish coast, studying face-to-face interaction in a crofting community. Alleging to be an American (he was to the end a Canadian) interested in agricultural techniques, Goffman studied the ways in which the islanders disclosed and hid information from each other. Working as a part-time assistant washer-up, he observed their everyday rituals and practices close up. With only 300 families on a small, flat island with almost no vegetation to partition the landscape, the crofters lived in almost continual sight of one another, and they became for Goffman a microcosm of society. With an elaborate set of definitions, classifications, and examples, he developed his field notes into a general account of face-to-face interaction. In contrast to the dry text of his Master's thesis, this work contains extended metaphors and sharp touches. Goffman returned to these ideas frequently in the ensuing years.

In 1956 the University of Edinburgh published his first book, *The Presentation of Self in Everyday Life*, which discussed a number of "dramaturgical principles". Each of these principles explores the social world as if it were a theatrical performance. The social world becomes filled with "impression management" and team performances, as each of us is transformed into a cynical role player who hides behind an array of performance masks. This image sharpens one contained both in parts of his doctoral thesis and in his earlier paper on the ways in which life is experienced as a confidence trick. Three years later, in 1959, *The Presentation of Self* was reissued by Penguin Press in Great Britain and by Anchor in the States. What had begun life as a relatively obscure research monograph was destined to become a bestseller. There are several changes to the second edition, which superficially appear only to amplify the initial themes. However, on closer inspection they have a corrosive quality, and ultimately undermine the coherence of the view that we are all cynical actors performing instrumentally for personal gain. Retrospectively, these appended passages to the second edition mark a subtle but important change in Goffman's ideas.

In the late 1950s and 1960s, Goffman pursued three interdependent projects, all involving the interpretation of everyday behavior. First, he produced work that appears to fall squarely into the sociology of deviance. In 1961, his extraordinary ethnography, *Asylums*, was published. This analyzes the experiences of inmates in a Washington mental institution, and by extension, in any institution in which the time and space of subordinates are carefully monitored and restricted. He called these places "total institutions", and his discussion of them helps us to understand the apparently irrational behavior of those who are held there. The four essays that make up this book combine extensive field observations with a dense knowledge of the scientific and popular literature. The result is an ethnography that is less a study of a specific hospital and more an ethnography of the concept of the total institution itself.

Goffman's second contribution to the sociology of deviance was called *Stigma* (1964a). Beginning with a poignant story of the hardships faced by a girl born without a nose, this book suggests that we are all stigmatized in some way: we are too fat, too short, we are losing our hair, we have failed in some activity in which we have invested a degree of self worth, etc. As a result, we have all learned to manage discrediting information about ourselves.

His second major project of the 1960s parallels his earlier work on the theatrical metaphor, only on this occasion he considered the social world not as theater but as a game. In *Encounters* (1961b) and *Strategic Interaction* (1970), he discusses everyday meetings as interactional "moves" enacted by players. This work leads Goffman to the edges of game and rational-choice theory; indeed, some of this work dates from his year spent with Thomas Schelling at Harvard. With characteristic imagination, Goffman draws upon an unusual source – true and fictional espionage stories – as a way of challenging our sense of what the mundane world is like. In this vein, he tells us that although to us a wrong number may be only a minor disruption to our day, to a spy it may cause anxiety and fear of disclosure. Our security in the fabric of the social world is not a natural feature of that world, but stems instead from a generally held set of rules of behavior. If we all lived our daily lives as spies, the social world would seem a frightening environment, where every meeting was a potential cause for fear. Of course, it is possible to see this erosion of trust in parts of cities such as New York. The key point is that we view these and similar locations as disturbing exceptions rather than as the norm. If the anxieties felt by many people in some parts of New York were typical of modern life, our experience of the social world would be radically different.

The third of Goffman's projects in the 1960s was the specification of the assumptions people use as they take part in social interaction. For most of us most of the time, the social world is predictable and routine. It is essential to see that this predictability is neither natural nor assured; instead it is an astonishing collective achievement to which we contribute daily in myriad ways. This means that the explanations of why, for example, kettles boil and cars stop at traffic lights must be quite separate. Goffman was quietly appalled by the number of methodologies that assume that people are comparable to inanimate objects. In the preface to *Relations in Public* (1971), for example, he suggests that sociologists who concentrate on hypothesis-testing are engaging in a type of "sympathetic magic" from which no knowledge of ordinary behavior can be gleaned. This type of research, he suggests, employs natural science analogs with only the hope that science will result (1971: 21).

Instead of viewing the predictability of social life as the consequence of underlying laws, Goffman thought that predictability was something that we all made happen; it is then, an issue of rule-following behavior. These rules of social interaction do not produce social order (they do not compel us to act); rather they are a way of exhibiting social order. Rules are subject to interpretation, to disagreement about what constitutes an occasion of rule-following, to exceptions, and to decisions not to abide by them. That the world is even in the slightest a predictable place is an extraordinary and largely invisible accomplishment.

Throughout the 1960s Goffman spent a considerable amount of time attempting to specify the broad assumptions people use in their everyday lives. By tracing a hesitant path through several of his books, it is possible to discern four basic assumptions, which I refer to as his SIAC schema. It is important to remember that Goffman did not use this acronym.

The first element of SIAC is "situational propriety". This suggests that the meaning of our actions is linked to the context in which they arose, and that we can rarely understand behavior without knowledge of the situation in which it occurred. If I ask someone to marry me, the significance of this act means one thing in a church and another in a theater.

Buried in his account is a critique of the mainstream American psychiatric practice of the 1950s, which had, Goffman thought, replaced a physiological explanation of different mental illnesses with a non-medical classification of socially unacceptable behavior. Goffman thought that situational improprieties reveal the structural obligations of social interaction. They uncover mixed motives, sometimes pointing to absent-mindedness, sometimes to feelings of alienation, frustration, antagonism, resentment, social incompetence, and sometimes to mental illness. Behavior which appears to indicate "madness" can on other occasions be perfectly understandable. For example, when a woman fails to respond to the questions of a psychiatrist, her behavior seems to be symptomatic of an underlying mental disorder; yet when the same woman shows indifference to the hoots, calls, and invitations of male adolescents, her actions seem well motivated and perfectly sane (1967: 146–7).

Goffman made several stabs at analytically distinguishing different types of context, and the ensuing constraints accompanying each. In doing so, he separated "encounters", in which there is a single focus of attention, from the "social occasions" in which they occur, and which are constrained by the event justifying their existence, such as a funeral or a New Year's Eve celebration. Social occasions can in turn be distinguished from "social gatherings", which are looser constellations of people, and "social situations", which Goffman used as a catch-all category for moments when any type of interpersonal monitoring can occur, such as in elevators or lobbies. His success in determining the different types of context and the different constraints operating in them remains to be seen, but he was surely correct to claim that some types of contextual constraints structure our understanding of everyday behavior.

The second element of SIAC is "involvement", which is our capacity to give, or to withhold from giving, concerted attention to the activity at hand (1963: 43). This idea originated in his doctorate, and, like much of his work, has a creeping effect: it begins as an innocuous observation but after a while it seems impossible to understand social life without it. In everyday interaction we are under pressure not simply to be involved in what's going on, but to be appropriately involved in the situation. For every encounter there is a degree of involvement which meets social demands and expectations. Daily activities correspond to an "involvement contour" of greater and lesser involvement, as when we move from a conversational encounter with an acquaintance to verbal exchanges in an important meeting. Failure to display the requisite response to a situation is likely to be sanctioned, and so we typically "shield" our actual level of involvement if it is inappropriate. For example, newspapers disguise our attentive eavesdropping of a nearby conversation. However flimsy the importance of involvement appears to be, it underwrites our general feeling that social world is a reliable and predictable place (Goffman, 1961a: 72).

The third and fourth elements of SIAC are "accessibility" and "civil inattention" and they are two sides of the same coin, since both concern the problem of participant ratification. In everyday life we allow ourselves to be accessible to all friends and "ratified" strangers, although exactly what it is that distinguishes ratified from unratified strangers is difficult to specify. We have the right to expect and a duty to give a host of minor courtesies to people – these include telling the time, giving directions or a match, etc. These keep us as members of a common social world which is more than just an aggregate of people. Our sensitivity to levels of interpersonal access is extraordinary: we reflexively monitor our surroundings, distinguishing friends, acquaintances, and strangers at some distance, often while managing hectic pedestrian traffic and a conversation. In fact, to ease pedestrian flow we usually all conspire to limit exchanges between friends to a brief moment. Thus, when walking down a street we will often see a friend in the distance; we then pretend not to have seen him or her until a moment before passing by – at which time the second of mutual accessibility can be filled with a smile and eye contact. By this deception we perform a ritual honor that both accommodates a busy schedule and avoids encounters in which appropriate involvement is difficult to sustain.

"Civil inattention" is the flip side of this: it involves both a willingness to be seen (hence it is a tacit statement that no aggression is intended) and a sign of deference to those present. Goffman's standard example of this is behavior in elevators. People struggle to avoid eye contact: they stare at their feet or the floor numbers as they ascend in what suddenly becomes a fascinating visual display. Civil inattention is the respect we owe to, and expect from, strangers. It is most poignantly brought to light in situations where it is withheld, as when a woman in a wheelchair enters a bar, orders a drink, and is met by a room of staring faces (this is a palimpsest of the B movie Western scene in which the piano player stops playing when the bad guy walks in).

From the 1970s until his death in 1982, Goffman worked on two further aspects of ordinary behavior. The first is a detailed exploration of how contexts structure our perceptions of the social world. Using an elaborate vocabulary to suggest that social life is "framed" in ways which specify the meaning of social situations, Goffman was able to identify how we routinely and effortlessly distinguish overall frames from frames-within-frames. If we were not able to distinguish the relationship between frames, we would be unable to interpret most everyday behavior. This is because we frequently "jump" from one frame to another, doing so in ways which are somehow identifiable and meaningful. For example, actors in commercials are sometimes scripted to remain on set to enjoy the products they have just promoted. Advertisers do this to manufacture a moment of sincerity, a jump to a new vantage point from which actors appear to be no longer acting (1974: 475).

Accompanying this emphasis on the framing of social life was the second development to this final period of his work. Building on the ideas of two of his former students, Harvey Sacks and Emanuel Schegloff, Goffman began to explore the organization of everyday talk. Prior to Sacks's seminal work with both Goffman and Garfinkel in the mid 1960s, no one appreciated how orderly mundane talk has to be in order to facilitate even quite small exchanges. For example, outbursts such as *"oops!"* seemed then (and seem now on first inspection) to be no more than background noises that obscure the meaning of ordinary talk. In fact, the reverse is the case: these apparent mistakes are essential organizing devices which are rich in meaning. These "spill-cries" have definite and specifiable meanings. Imagine spilling a drink and not saying *"oops!"*; or conversely, imagine saying *"oops!"* as a friend tripped and fell off a cliff. In this case, the situational impropriety could easily be heard as a sign of mental illness.

To talk about the apparent paradox that we can somehow "know" what spill-cries mean without being able to explain them, we need a conceptual refinement that is missing from Goffman's work but which has been supplied by Giddens, who distinguishes "practical" from "discursive" consciousness. The former holds information that we can't explain in words, the latter information that we can (Giddens, 1984).

Many of the details of formal and informal conversations can be shown to be quite mechanical; that is to say, composed of identifiable procedures for completing various interactional tasks. We have devices for beginning phone conversations that tell callers about the location of the number they've just called (whether it's an office or a private home, for example); we also have devices for ending phone calls (it's almost impossible to end calls by simply saying "goodbye"). In a similar vein, there are identifiable mechanisms for introducing topics into conversations, for affirming levels of intimacy, initiating laughter, and so on. However trivial this game appears to be, it structures our view of the social world, and we spend our lives playing it (Goffman, 1981a: 327).

## A Summary of Goffman's Methods

Discounting his pre-doctoral use of statistics, Goffman's methods fall into three categories:

1 extended metaphorical description;
2 unsystematic, naturalistic observation;
3 systematic naturalistic observation (ethnography).

None of these categories is self-explanatory, and Goffman often used several of these approaches at the same time. Since some of combinations of them are contradictory, he sometimes appeared to speak with different "voices". His and our failure to discern these different research strategies has been a major hurdle to an adequate appreciation of his ideas.

Goffman's first research strategy was to use extended metaphors, normally those of life as theater and as game. His insight was to see that metaphors did not have to be treated as either appendages to research projects or as pithy ways of exemplifying their claims. Instead, a metaphor can be used as an idiosyncratic map to the social world. This implies that throw-away comments such as "he's just playing a role" can be shown to be part of a wider vocabulary that can redescribe social phenomena. Thus, the apparently mundane spatial organization of restaurants or corporate offices can be reconsidered as carefully partitioned "front" and "backstages". By using the subjunctive mood extensively, Goffman was able to make everyday events look very mysterious.

The reasons why this is possible are instructive: despite their literal absurdity, Goffman's metaphors are meant to be understood, i.e. they point to forms of interpretation already within our horizon of possibility. Unlike a metaphor which may indicate, for example, that the social world is a banana, theatrical and game metaphors strike a sympathetic chord: although they are challenging, they are also imaginable. The problem with research based on extended metaphors is that they are difficult to substantiate. What credibility have research projects that "invest" heavily in one or other metaphor? When sociology relies on the ideas generated by distinctive metaphors, the discipline begins to look like a version of literature (as Cioffi has suggested), and as we will see, in his later writings Goffman tried to produce a more formal account of the organization of everyday experience than this approach allows.

Goffman's second strategy was to gather observations of face-to-face interaction from his own life and organize these into general descriptions. I call this "spiraling" research for reasons that will become apparent later. Robin Williams (1988), using some ideas of Baldamus (1977), calls the same strategy "reciprocal double fitting". The general idea is that although research projects are always vulnerable to exceptional cases, these exceptions can be treated as strengths rather than as weaknesses. Instead of devising explanations of social phenomena, trying to falsify them, and then discarding failures, Goffman focused on what the vulnerabilities or limitations of any model could tell us about the organization of the social world. In a sentence, he made a compromise between conceptual elegance and loyalty to empirical detail: sometimes he accommodated discrepant data by altering his analytic framework, sometimes he just ignored discrepancies.

In his later work, Goffman tried to produce a "metaschema" for the interpretation of everyday life. This can be seen at many points in both *Frame Analysis* (1974) and *Forms of Talk* (1981a), where he almost analyzes the social world as if he were going to program computers to take part in it. But we can only say "almost", because he accompanied this idea of social-life-as-computer-program with passages that ridicule such a project, proclaiming instead that social life is an inexhaustible and non-formalizable "Pandora's box" of possibilities.

Nevertheless, Goffman's interest in the extent to which everyday interaction could be reduced to a computer program spans his career, and it is worth noting that it is an interest that he thinks brings him intellectually close to Harold Garfinkel. For example, in his essay, "Mental Symptoms and Public Order", first published in 1964 and reprinted in *Interaction Ritual* (1967), he cites approvingly Garfinkel's suggestion that it should be possible to "program insanity, that is, reduce to a minimum the instructions you would have to give an experimental subject in order to enable him to act crazy, from within as it were" (1967: 140). This same thought appears again in *Frame Analysis* (1974: 5), where he again cites Garfinkel and again refers to the possibilities of demonstrating that the meaningfulness of activity may be reducible to a closed and finite set of rules (a computer algorithm).

Goffman's third research strategy was ethnography. Aside from his pre-doctoral sortie with service-station dealers, he also conducted ethnographic research on a Shetland island for his dissertation, in a Washington hospital and a Las Vegas casino. Information on this last project is sketchy: it is cited in his work but never published separately.

As suggested earlier, the key to understanding his ethnographies is to see them as ethnographies of concepts rather than of places. They are utopian ideal-types (such as the total institution) existing nowhere (Weber, 1949: 98). Goffman studied these concepts by tracing the schematic resemblances between different examples of his basic model – typically he did this by merging his own field notes with a rather eclectic database of other ethnographies, journalistic pieces, and autobiographies. Throughout, his intention was to devise new vocabularies with which to redescribe overfamiliar events.

One of the difficulties in reading Goffman is that he frequently shifts between these methodological strategies, insisting on the necessity of each of them at certain moments, ridiculing each of them at others. Throughout his work he remained committed to game and theatrical metaphors, to ethnographic and spiraling research and to the hope of programming computers to simulate human responses (i.e. for them to pass the Turing test). However, he also routinely pointed to the limitations of metaphorical interpretations of the social world, he frequently replaced ethnographic data with contrived examples, and he spent a hot of time ridiculing mechanistic accounts of human behavior. To his supporters, these contradictions are essential parts of his enigmatic mastery of sociology; to his critics they are just inconsistencies.

A significant part of this book will be spent clarifying and detailing Goffman's ideas. However, the book also has two other goals: to form bridges between Goffman, symbolic interactionism, and ethnomethodology, and to show why these ideas are an inescapable part of most attempts to practice sociology. I now want to consider briefly both of these remaining questions.

## GOFFMAN AND MICROSOCIOLOGY

Goffman's work has similarities with both symbolic interactionism and ethnomethodology. Let me say a word about each. The term "symbolic interactionism" was coined by Herbert Blumer in an essay published in 1937. The term was well received, and began to represent the different types of sociology that rely on participant observation and field research. In 1969, Blumer published *Symbolic*

*Interactionism*, which contained a detailed exposition of this perspective. Claiming an impressive intellectual foundation in the work of Mead, Dewey, Park, William James, and others, Blumer synthesized their varied contributions into three "premises" and six "root images". Put simply, and briefly, the three premises suggest that social action is based on the meanings we attribute to them, that meanings are derived from social interaction, and that these are modified in the course of social interaction (1969: 2). The six root images suggest that society is an aggregate of individual performances, that social interaction is central to any definition of society, that objects are the product of interpretations, and that social life is purposeful, interpretive, and interlinked (1969: 6–21).

One of the problems of Blumer's characterization of symbolic interactionism is that almost all sociologists agree with his premises and root images (their disagreements are to be found elsewhere). Shortly before his death, Goffman was asked whether he saw himself as a symbolic interactionist, and replied that the label was too vague to do much work (quoted in Winkin, 1988: 235–6).

During his graduate studies at Chicago, Goffman obtained a working knowledge of Simmel's ideas, and these serve as a mandate for the detailed study of everyday life. For Goffman, Simmel exemplified symbolic interactionism. Central to Simmel's sociology is the problematic nature of description: because social life is in a state of constant flux it is remarkably difficult to describe. In the midst of this flux, phenomena mutually affect each other, with the result that apparently small actions prove to be highly consequential and no element can be known in advance to be trivial. Simmel explained this in a passage which Goffman placed at the front of his doctoral thesis. In it he compares society to the human body, arguing that the study of the State, religion, and the family are comparable to the medical study of the heart, lungs, and major organs. But, he claims, although these elements are indispensable to the healthy functioning of the body and society respectively, so too are a multitude of innumerable unknown or unnamed "tissues":

> ... the interactions we have in mind when we talk about "society" are crystallized as definable, consistent structures such as the state and the family, the guild and the church, social classes and organizations based on common interests.
>
> But in addition to these, there exists an immeasurable number of less conspicuous forms of relationship and kinds of interaction. Taken singly, they may appear negligible. But since in actuality they are inserted into more comprehensive and, as it were, official social formations, they alone produce society as we know it. To confine ourselves to the large social formations resembles the older science of anatomy with its limitation to the major, definitely circumscribed organs such as heart, liver, lungs and stomach, and with its neglect of the immeasurable, popularly unnamed or unknown tissues. Yet without these, the more obvious organs could never constitute a living organism. (Simmel, 1950: 9; quoted in Goffman 1953b: iv)

Goffman viewed his work as an appendage to this "manifesto" about the importance of unnoticed facets of the social world. Simmel's insight was to see that projects claiming to have discovered underlying determinants to everyday behavior grant quasi-causal priority in advance to one or other element of social organization (such as the State or class structure). As a result, they reduce the actual complexity of the social world to a level compatible with their own analytic limits. By contrast, Simmel used metaphor to cast incongruous insights onto problems. Metaphor discloses a descriptive labyrinth of possibilities in which the only certainty is the unendingly provisional character of the ensuing research.

Simmel advocates descriptions of the apparently banal events and exchanges that maintain social organization. These are the "unnamed or unknown tissues" of the social body. This biological metaphor undermines traditional hierarchies in the social sciences, which he likens to the outmoded predispositions of anatomy. Macro-sociological thinking, which he disparagingly calls the "the traditional subject matter of social science", has trivialized the problem of sociological description. Both Simmel and Goffman use these arguments to justify their use of fantastically diverse databases, made up of scholarly texts, novels, newspaper cuttings (Simmel was himself also a journalist), personal observations, empirical studies, made-up examples, and even radio "bloopers". Both writers show that many types of data can be instructive guides to the structure of everyday experience.

Simmel and Goffman's methodology is, as Williams argues (1983, 1988), a neo-Kantian one that is closely allied to that of Max Weber. Sociological investigations comprise ideal-types, each of which is a one-sided accentuation of one or more points of view (Weber, 1949: 90). They are abstractions or composites, culled from a great many actually existing phenomena. They are not descriptions of reality, but they aid description – they are "utopian" – existing nowhere. In Simmel's example, the "Gothic style" is an abstraction which is obtained from many examples but which designates none of them (1950: 5–6). Ideal-types are perspectives that are partial and transient because the "eternally onward flowing stream of culture perpetually brings new problems" (Weber, 1949: 104). Each perspective makes an arbitrary cut into its subject matter – a point Goffman reminds us of in the prefaces to most of his books. Both Simmel and Goffman refuse to treat empirical detail as merely the residue of theoretical schemata. Like Weber, they are "analytic dualists", believing that sociological knowledge is unavoidably a simplification of the unmanageable complexity of the social world (Williams, 1983).

A second important strand in Simmel's elusive and complex writings is an embryonic theory of modernity which is only assumed by Goffman in his own work. Simmel's analyses show that the small interpersonal rituals of everyday life are not only intricate, they are also quite dis-

tinctively modern. These rituals are some of the unnamed
or unknown tissues which help constitute our familiar
experiences of contemporary society. Perhaps this view
is most evident in his *Philosophy of Money*, where he
shows in considerable detail that the anonymity of capital
is mirrored by the anonymity of everyday encounters.
This is simultaneously a possible source of Durkheimian
anomie, Marxian exploitation, and a distinctively modern
from of freedom, exemplified by the blasé attitude of the
urban commuter in Simmel's "Metropolis" essay. One of
Simmel's central insights was that this economic and interpersonal development of anonymity does not necessarily
lead to a general ethos of cynical manipulation; instead it
frequently leads to the development of quite distinctive
conditions of trust. Thus he writes:

> Our modern life is based to a much larger extent than is
> usually realized upon the faith in the honesty of the other.
> Examples are our economy, which becomes more and more
> a credit economy, or our science, in which most scholars
> must use innumerable results of others scientists which
> they cannot examine. We base our gravest decisions on a
> complex system of conceptions, most of which presuppose
> the confidence that we will not be betrayed. Under modern
> conditions, the lie, therefore, becomes something much
> more devastating than it was earlier, something which ques-
> tions the very foundations of our life. If among ourselves
> today, the lie were as negligible as it was among the Greek
> Gods, the Jewish patriarchs, or the South Seas islanders;
> and if we were not deterred from it by the utmost severity
> of the moral law; then the organization of modern life
> would be simply impossible; for modern life is a "credit
> economy" in a much broader than a strictly economic sense.
> (1950: 313)

Simmel analyzed the apparent paradox that the development of conditions of anonymity is accompanied by elaborate conditions of trust in a variety of settings, showing, for
example, that even – perhaps especially – secret societies

provide a "very impressive schooling" in the necessity of "moral solidarity" (1950: 348–51).

Substantively, then, modern social practices offer a reliable sense of form that underwrites the fragmentary social flux with patterns of reliable and courteous behavior. Simmel calls this the "sociability drive", linking our understanding of forms of sociability to a moral understanding of "good form" (1950: 44). It turns aggregates of people into regulated gatherings and in time into little social worlds.

Before I leave Goffman and symbolic interactionism and turn to his relationship with ethnomethodology, a summary word may be useful. Blumer's specifications of symbolic interactionism distinguish sociologists who take social action as constitutive of society from those who don't. Goffman thought that this was too general a distinction, and, aside from supporting the use of role analytic terms, he otherwise saw himself as outside of this school. The way to synthesize Goffman and symbolic interactionism is to include Simmel as a founding father, and to then draw on both his methodological insight about the problematic nature of sociological description and his substantive insight that sociologists should study the essential but unnamed tissues of the social body. These tissues are, it transpires, the subject matter of both Goffman and the symbolic interactionists. With that, let me turn to ethnomethodology.

Garfinkel's curious term, which he first coined in the 1950s, directs our attention to the ways in which we all reason about what the world is like. He tells us that he thought of the term while browsing through file catalogs at Yale University library; although the inspiration for the term actually derives from a collaborative study he worked on concerning the ways in which jurors reach their verdicts. Garfinkel came to believe that a central dilemma for jurors was the distinction between how they reached decisions in their everyday lives and how they were expected to reach decisions in a court of law. For example, jurors want to know the difference between a "fact" in everyday life and a legal "fact". In short, they want to know the methods they are to use in order to "do" the task of being a juror (Garfinkel, 1974: 15–18).

It is quite common for ethnomethodologists to talk about doing rather than being something: they write papers with titles such as "Doing Friendship' or 'Doing Shyness" (although I've invented these examples). Their point is that there are identifiable ways by which such activities are accomplished or achieved. For example, from an ethnomethodological point of view, shyness is neither a good nor a bad thing, nor is it a sign that the person is socially handicapped. On the contrary, shyness is a remarkable social accomplishment, requiring many skills. A shy person must be able to resist invitations to speak or continue speaking, avoid eye contact with would-be socializers, etc. Shyness involves subtle manipulations to the turn-taking system of everyday talk, careful body alignment, and many other accomplishments. The subtlety of these performances is extraordinary.

Ethnomethodologists believe that we have to deploy these methods and exhibit practical reasoning in order to get through our daily lives. For every task, whether ending a telephone conversation or ordering a cheeseburger, we make use of specifiable procedures which are similar to the algorithms computer scientists use to program computers. Consider ending a phone conversation: most of us like to think that we do so in quite spontaneous ways, but ethnomethodologists have been able to show that there are quite definite and identifiable methods for ending a phone call. Often we implicitly negotiate the end of a phone call by reconfirming a prior arrangement; for example, if we've been talking on the phone for a while and I say "so I'll see you on Friday at noon", this comment is heard not as a request for confirmation of a forthcoming event, but as a polite way of inviting the end of the phone call. Ethnomethodologists explain these issues in much greater detail (see Schegloff and Sacks, 1984). We could wonder what type of interaction we engage in without these procedures.

The implications of the phone argument are already being tested empirically at a research laboratory at MIT, where they are developing a new kind of answering machine that doesn't merely take messages, it also "talks" to the caller using a microchip of the owner's voice hooked up to programs for doing phone calls (see Brand, 1987).

A central question for ethnomethodology, artificial intelligence, and Goffman is the extent to which these implicit interactional programs can be manipulated by individuals for their own purposes. Human creativity, as Douglas Hofstadter suggests, can be understood as the capacity to make variations on themes, in this case, inter-actional themes. Garfinkel refers to this creativity as "ad hocing" and sees it as a vital interactional resource; other ethnomethodologists are much more concerned with social life as a set of relatively fixed procedures. These prob-lems center on the issue of rule-following in everyday life. What is the most appropriate definition of a rule? The difficulty is to find a way of acknowledging that although rules guide our actions, they do not determine what we do. For example, there is an informal rule that strangers shouldn't talk to each other, but there are acceptable ways of circumventing this rule, as when someone asks a stranger for a "free supply", such as the time.

In later chapters I will suggest that we have three broad ideas about rules. The first idea is that rules are instruc-tions about what to do (and what not to do) in certain situations. The second idea is that rules are background assumptions about the range of behavior to expect. The third idea is that one rule underpins all other rules: this is the requirement to demonstrate the sanity behind our actions. Goffman referred to this requirement as "Felicity's Condition". I will return to these important questions later in the book, most of which owe an important debt to ethnomethodological concerns. This section has certainly been an esoteric route through their ideas.

## GOFFMAN'S CONTRIBUTION TO MODERN SOCIOLOGY

Goffman has generally been considered to be either an empiricist with a sharp eye or an exponent of symbolic interactionism. In the first case, he has often been considered insufficiently theoretical; in the second as just the representative of a school. In fact, it is clear that Goffman's work is theoretically sophisticated, if somewhat inconsistent, and that his ideas are not identical with any one school. Nevertheless, there is common ground between Goffman and many other microsociologists. This common ground must be emphasized so that it can be used in a range of sociological projects that lie outside the immediate field of face-to-face interaction.

If there is a sense of "crisis" within sociology, it is linked to the difficulties of uniting theoretical and empirical work. One of the perennial problems with social theory has been its relative failure to produce ideas that can be operationalized. Too often theory is interesting but inapplicable. This is because, unlike empirical studies which at least make tacit use of some lay knowledge about what the social world is like, social theory has often been indifferent to everyday knowledge. Without it theory can only generate models of societies in which, paradoxically, there seem to be no people.

Whenever social scientists attempt to assess the implications of any structural transformations to a society, it is essential for them to consider the ramifications of these transformations for our experience of everyday life. Then the apparent differences between the "theoretical" and the "empirical" or the "macro" and "micro" become only different "moments" in sociological research.

Rather than pursuing this at length here, let me offer a vignette instead. Consider the large number of social scientists who are concerned with urban planning. The photographs of urban landscapes used by both urban planners and architects rarely contain any of the people who are to live in or use the urban space they depict. It is as if they were insignificant details in the design. Arguably, many of the blunders of urban design, such as undesirable apartment buildings, could have been avoided by an awareness of the SIAC schema. An awareness of the importance of civil inattention and involvement contours makes certain types of urban design seem not merely foolhardy but immediately doomed. Like us, urban planners have often been so familiar with the rules concerning everyday conduct that they have taken them to be completely inconsequential, and yet without spatial arrangements facilitating the easy maintenance of these rules, the social world becomes a terrifying and unpredictable place.

William H. Whyte (1988) has written persuasively about the lack of insight which has accompanied the use of space in many downtown American cities. In fact, with the aid of detailed research, he has been able to convince the State of New York to act upon some of this guidelines for the construction of new buildings. And of course, comments that apply to urban design also apply to many other fields of social research.

An understanding of Goffman's ideas and those of allied schools of thought will deepen our understanding of how the social world is experienced and reproduced. This understanding is vital to our efforts to improve our institutions and social environment, whether as urban planners, politicians, social scientists, or citizens.

# 2
# Early Writings

## Introduction

In this chapter I consider Goffman's predoctoral writings, his dissertation and both editions of *The Presentation of Self in Everyday Life* (1956a, 1959). By the time that the second and better-known edition of *The Presentation of Self* was published in 1959, many of the now familiar themes of Goffman's sociology had emerged: by then he had shown himself to be an accomplished ethnographer, he had established face-to-face interaction as his principal research interest, he had displayed a formidable talent for defining and classifying complex phenomena with a range of elegant expressions, and he had entertained the thought that we can be both cynical manipulators of social situations and trusting individuals with an implicit faith in a social contract of mutual help.

His later work contains a series of refinements to this basic set of ideas. Thus, *Asylums* is methodologically superior to his ethnographically oriented Ph.D., "Communication Conduct in an Island Community"; his writings in the 1960s and 1970s are a more sophisticated analysis of the rules of social interaction than his earlier attempts, and overall his work focuses on the ways in which we are guardians of a precarious social order. In this chapter, then, we see the themes of Goffman's later work in their embryonic form.

In the 1950s his work offers two accounts of the self, one emphasizing cynicism, the other trust and ritual. The first account was influenced by theatrical and game metaphors, the second by Durkheim's ideas about social solidarity.

Goffman's use of the theatrical metaphor questioned the idea of personal identity. Etymologically, the person is a "mask" and the ensuing implication is that the "real" person is hidden behind a mask or set of masks. This imagery suggests that we cynically select masks to impress our various audiences. There is an intuitive appeal to this analysis that is supported by our frequent talk about efforts to find out what someone is "really like". However, during his early work, Goffman became deeply suspicious of this intuitive view, even though it saturated his own analyses of everyday life. When the opportunity arose in the late 1950s to revise the first edition of *The Presentation of Self*, he did so by appending passages to some of the chapters of this book that quietly undermine this cynical view of self. By so doing, he drew to a close his early interest in the cynicism of everyday behavior and the use of extended theatrical descriptions of social life. This led him back to his interest in the ritual preservation of face evident in other predramaturgical papers.

Before turning to *The Presentation of Self* I want to look at the papers and projects which preceded it. These show him oscillating between cynical and ritual interpretations of social life, his developing style, and his wide range of empirical interests.

## THE SERVICE-STATION DEALER

Goffman's first ethnography is an unpublished report called, "The Service Station Dealer: The Man and His

Work". It was commissioned by the American Petroleum Institute and completed in February 1953, nine months before his dissertation was formally accepted by the University of Chicago. The report (which runs to about 100 pages) analyzes the conflicting roles and aspirations of service-station dealers – men who either owned or leased petrol stations. In a manner reminiscent of his Master's thesis, "Some Characteristics of Response to Depicted Experience" (1949), he triangulated data, using statistical information, structured and unstructured interviews, and ethnographic observations. His findings were gleaned from information about 204 petrol stations in and around Chicago.

The crux of the report is that dealers have three main roles: business man, service attendant, and technician. All three are in conflict. As business man the dealer is relatively independent and prestigious, as service attendant he is at everyone's beck and call – wiping windshields, brushing cars, etc. (1953a: 7). As technician his status is harder to assign, because although the role involves expert knowledge (and expertise is normally prestigious), the knowledge in question is practical and hence downgraded.

In his subsequent discussions of the positive and negative factors of their work, these three roles lurk in the background, identifiable in discussions of topics as diverse as abstract claims of independence and concrete complaints about bad weather. Typically the dealer is ambivalent about his roles, especially that of businessman, which brings with it the mixed blessings of prestige and financial worry and responsibility. The dealers are often isolated from the local business community and their prestige, it transpires, is rather hollow (1953a: 54).

In contrast to their hazy sense of their own independence, they are much clearer about their everyday categorizations. Thus, on the question of the difference between good and bad customers, they consistently outlined the bad customer as one who acts in a superior way, expects too much service, doesn't respect the professional authority of the dealer, wants credit, complains about the price (whatever the price is), tries to cheat the dealer, expects "freebies", free technical help, and treats the petrol station as public space rather than as private property (1953a: 37–9). Good customers are considerate, allow a personal relationship to develop between themselves and the dealer, acknowledge his desired status, and show a loyalty to him. They also buy liberally from the station shop and allow the dealer to use discretion when servicing their cars (1953a: 40).

Although of some interest, this report lacks the wit, sociological backdrop, methodological sensitivity, and inspired footnoting of *The Presentation of Self* and thereafter. The elements of the report that are characteristic of his later work are the emphasis on taxonomy, the specification of the everyday knowledge of the dealer, and the focus on general role characteristics rather than on biographical evidence. Nevertheless, it is not an obvious forerunner to *The Presentation of Self* and he rarely referred to the report in his later work. The study is a learning exercise and contributes only marginally to our understanding of what is distinctive about Goffman's sociology. For this we must turn to his dissertation.

## THE DISSERTATION: "COMMUNICATION CONDUCT IN AN ISLAND COMMUNITY"

Using the findings of twelve months' extensive research, the dissertation describes the day-to-day lives of the inhabitants of a small island (called Dixon) off the coast of Scotland. Throughout the study there is an unresolved tension between the construction of general (if not universal) frameworks and the observation of the minutiae of everyday life on the island. It is probably his awareness of this tension that singles out his work from the mainstream of Chicago urban ethnography, and is the first clue to the distinctiveness of his approach. Unlike the theses of his Chicago colleagues, such a Taxel (1953), Willoughby (1953), and Habenstein (1954), which closely observed a single setting, Goffman set out with the ambition of constructing general classifications of face-to-face interaction.

This ambition explains the curious status he accords observation, which is neither sufficiently detailed nor well-enough located to be interesting in its own right. Its significance is part of a much more general ambition to classify types of social behavior while remaining sensitive to the complexity of everyday life.

The dissertation contains five sections: Part 1 describes Dixon, Part 2 presents a conceptual model, Part 3 analyzes the management of information about oneself, Part 4 proposes a schema of units of interaction and Part 5 deals directly with the crofters' conversational techniques. The dissertation ends with some broad conclusions and tentative suggestions for future research.

The Introduction tells us that the aim of the thesis is to develop a "general communication framework" (1953b: 9). The suspicion this raises is that the empirical sections of the thesis are inserted as a post facto justification for an a priori schema. Goffman emphasized that this was not the case ("I should like to make it clear that the terms and concepts employed in this study came after and not before the facts" (1953b: 9)).

The dissertation begins quietly with a description of Dixon and its inhabitants. Dixon is one of a cluster of islands about 100 miles off the Scottish coast. It is a rectangular piece of rock, 9 miles long and 4 miles wide, covered with a thin layer of poor top soil. At the time of the study, 300 (exclusively white) people lived on the island. Goffman divided them into two groups: the Public School educated "gentry" and the rest – the "locals". This division was used routinely by the islanders themselves (1953b: 16). Dixon possessed two gentry families (the Squire's family and the Doctor's); the rest of the islanders were crofters. Dixon was flat with little vegetation and as a result the islanders were frequently (and potentially, always) able to monitor each other.

The second section of the thesis presents a theoretical overview. This is the only such statement in his entire corpus and it begins with the claim that the bulk of the later work attempts to document – that "conversational interaction between concrete persons who are in each other's immediate presence is a species of social order" (1953b: 33). Goffman used the following model of social order:

1  social order exists once social action is integrated in the pursuit of goals;
2  behavior is constrained by expectations that are generally held to be legitimate;
3  behavior is positively sanctioned;
4  social order is regulated by a wider context;
5  rule-following behavior is enforced by interactional pressures;
6  rule-breaking renders offenders deviant;
7  rule-breaking should lead to feelings of remorse in the offenders and indignation in the offended;
8  remedial work follows rule-breaking. (1953b: 33–6)

He was unhappy about the vagueness of this account of social order, and it sits uneasily next to his sensitive handling of empirical material later in the dissertation. In particular, he felt that this model undervalues "a crucial characteristic of conversational interaction". As it stands, the model focuses on the strategic quality of social life, a militaristic metaphor that prompted him to suggest that social interaction is "not a scene of harmony" but an "arrangement for pursuing a cold war" (1953b: 40).

Part 3 of the dissertation analyzes the management of information about oneself. Central to this section is an uneasy distinction between "expressive" and "instrumental" behavior (1953b: 50). Behavior is expressive when the actor's character overflows into his or her actions, it is instrumental to the extent that it is a means to an end. This distinction is, however, only an analytic one: in practice the two elements coexist in interactional exchanges. Goffman suggested that expressive behavior is necessarily vague, non-discursive, uncalculated, and inseparable from its transmission (1953b: 69–70). It is a wild card in the everyday game of information and impression management, adding uncertainty to the constant conversational game of "concealment and search" (1953b: 84).

Up to this point, the dissertation promotes, implicitly or explicitly, a game-theoretic account of social life. According to this view, we are all playing tactically and strategically to outwit rivals in the pursuit of personal gain. For Goffman, the implication of both theatrical and game metaphors is that cynicism and hidden motives underlie human behavior. However, although much of his dissertation defends this account, it also strikes a blow against it. The decisive moment occurs when his analysis spirals away from game theory to explore the implications of observations that resist a game theoretic classification. The area of social life that remains unaccounted for by game theory is that of ritual.

For sociology, ritual is an essential corrective to game theory and with this newly discovered focus Goffman's project takes a Durkheimian turn:

> The social attributes of recipients must be constantly honored; where these attributes have been dishonored, propitiation must follow. The actor . . . must conduct himself with great ritual care, threading his way through one situation, avoiding another, counteracting a third, lest he unintentionally and unwittingly convey a judgment of those present that is offensive to them. Even more that being a game of informational management, conversational interaction is a problem if ritual management. (1953b: 103)

This thought allows him to end the third section with the following allusion to the Durkheim of *The Elementary*

*Forms*: "An idol is to a person as a rite is to etiquette" (1953b: 104). Etiquette is the islanders' right to expect unquestioned access to each other; it is a bond of allegiance, revealing one of the ways that the *conscience collective* limits game-theoretic approaches to social life (1953b: 183–207).

The fourth part of the thesis attempts to categorize units of conversational interaction by establishing a basic model of communication. The model is that of a sender sending a message to a recipient, the message being the meanings and the vehicles that carry them. Goffman's interest in this model derives from the indeterminacy of the message's meaning, which must be "posted", relinquished to a vehicle for transportation. The vehicle codifies the message in a manner that prevents the original, authentic meaning from being retrieved. This Saussurian argument has been analyzed very carefully by the French thinker, Jacques Derrida, in a series of works ranging from investigations of Husserl to a fascinating and often funny edition of "postcards" sent to a Parisian lover (Derrida, 1987).

Matters are further complicated by context – the space through which the vehicle transports the message. This space profoundly affects meaning. Consider one example, "social occasions": these specify rules of participation, they have a beginning, an end, and an "involvement contour" – a predictable line of high and low points of involvement. Goffman argued that conversational exchanges can only be understood against this backdrop (1953b: 134). Messages don't travel through a vacuum: they are affected by both contextual constraints and the varying "participation statuses" of the speakers and hearers. This argument suggests that sociologists must understand how meaning is constrained by context.

The fifth and final part of the thesis analyzes conduct during interactional exchanges, distinguishing "euphoric" from "dysphoric" occasions (1953b: 243). Euphoria occurs when exchanges run smoothly, with little or no embarrassment or self-consciousness; dysphoria occurs when exchanges are derailed. Contextual norms govern appropriate levels of euphoria. For example, there are clearly occasions when one should appear embarrassed or self-conscious and not to be so indicates a "faulty person", to use Goffman's term.

A constant problem for interactants is to generate appropriate levels of euphoria. This typically takes the form of appropriate levels of involvement. The ideal that much of social life is spent trying to appear suitably involved or detached is developed in his later work, especially in *Behavior in Public Places* (1963a) and *Relations in Public* (1971). The dissertation only signposts this avenue, continuing the argument by considering the ways in which tacit restrictions stop the exploitation of people donating their involvement to encounters. Goffman discussed six types of exploitation and the sanctions that combat them. They analyze the tension between speakers' efforts to impress their listeners, and the requirement that they appear selfless (1953b: 253–84). In return, listeners should and do conspire to protect speakers against attack or ridicule. Goffman's interactional game of "concealment and search" is also a game of tact and beyond that it is a game of tact about tact, a point returned to in *The Presentation of Self* (1959: 225).

"Communication Conduct" offers three broad directives for sociology: it should maintain a tension between general and specific pronouncements about social organization, it should show the ways in which game-theoretic behavior is tempered by ritual constraints, and it should offer procedural guides to conduct which outline the context of rule-following practices. These ideas (and the database out of which they arose) remained a central resource for Goffman throughout his work.

The implications of the game and theater metaphors are similar: both suggest that we are cynical manipulators of social situations. In "Communication Conduct" Goffman traced this argument through the game metaphor, reaching the conclusion that the metaphor hides the importance

of the ritualistic elements of everyday life. This conclusion is important substantively because it extends our
understanding beyond the limits set by this metaphor. It
is important methodologically because it shows that the
limitations or partiality of metaphors can be transformed
into strengths rather than weaknesses. This is because they
allow us "to play the world twice", first metaphorically and
then in ways initially obscured by metaphor.

## PREPARATIONS FOR THE DRAMATURGICAL PERSPECTIVE

The fluency of the second edition (1959) of *The Presentation
of Self* can obscure the fact that it was the outcome of
decade's work. In 1949 he presented "Symbols of Class
Status" to the annual meeting of the University of Chicago
Society for Social Research and two years later a modified
version was published in the *British Journal of Sociology*.
This paper shows Goffman exploring a problem that exists
in the still waters at the edge of the dramaturgical mael-
strom. The crux of the paper is that although symbols of
class status represent status, they do not constitute it.
This discrepancy directs attention towards both fraudulent
presentations of self and towards the attempts of legitimate
status holders to immunize their symbols against misuse.
Goffman explicated the importance of these symbols in
Durkheimian terms, arguing that they affirm the traditions
and moral values of a community (1951: 294–6). He
believed that although these symbols are protected by
"curator groups", there is nevertheless a "circulation of
symbols" among modern consumers, during which their
uniqueness is obliterated (1951: 301–4). Paradoxically,
the effort by a community to adopt new and "untainted"
symbols serves only to undermine the traditions they are
meant to affirm. The way in which this argument challenges

our sense of authenticity has a distinctly postmodern element.

The "Symbols" paper does not draw explicitly on the theater analogy but it does raise questions about the necessary conditions for authentic presentations of self. A second paper, "On Cooling the Mark Out," published in *Psychiatry* in 1952, comes closer to this topic. Drawing on the idiom of confidence tricksters, Goffman discussed the cynical manipulations of everyday performances in the pursuit of profit. The metaphor implies that the social world consists of "con artists" and their "marks", the former giving the latter "instruction in the philosophy of taking a loss" (1952: 452). Goffman suggested that in everyday life we are all self-consciously "marked" men and women, conducting our activities to minimize the risk of being "conned" and of subsequently having to be "cooled out"; that is, of having to be reconciled to the "death" of one of our social selves (1952: 462). In a memorable image he suggested that modern societies do not segregate the dead, but allow them to continue to walk among the living (1952: 463).

In two other predramaturgical papers Goffman argued against cynical interpretations of social behavior, emphasizing instead the importance of ritual constraints. Randall Collins (1988) has revealed the extent to which Goffman's early work is "a continuation of the Durkheimian tradition" (1988: 43). This commitment to Durkheim is especially evident in two papers, "On Face-work" (1955, reprinted in Goffman, 1967), and "Embarrassment and Social Organization" (1956c, reprinted in Goffman, 1967). Instead of analyzing people as calculative manipulators seeking personal gain, these papers suggest that we are all guardians of face-to-face situations. The motive for behavior is no longer to maximize personal gain but to protect social situations.

In all social situations individuals are obliged to project a self that has a "positive social value". This image of self is a person's "face", and we try hard to protect it. There is a general conspiracy to save face so that social situations can also be saved: loss of face at a party, business luncheon, or even casual meeting undermines the entire event. The desire to save the face of others leads to tactful behavior, the desire to save our own leads us to monitor our actions carefully: "Approved attributes and their relation to face make of every man his own jailer; this is a fundamental social constraint even though each man may like his cell" (1967: 10). Face-work makes our actions consistent with our projected selves. Consistency is maintained either through avoidance or through corrective actions, the success of the former making the latter redundant. The result of face-work is self-regulating interaction that sustains a "ritual equilibrium" (1967: 45).

Goffman's analysis of embarrassment is a logical continuation of this argument: embarrassment occurs whenever a projected self cannot be sustained. The fact that we are not constantly embarrassed is testimony to both the strength of the ritual order and the prevalence of tact. We routinely exaggerate our own importance in ways that could make loss of face a common problem. It isn't, and loss of face only occurs when the gap between projected and actual self is unbridgeable (1967: 111).

Goffman's predramaturgical writings emphasized that both cynicism and trust are displayed in everyday encounters. *The Presentation of Self*, however, focuses primarily on cynicism and largely ignores trust. In his later work he threads a route back from the immorality of the confidence trick to the necessary conditions for trust in everyday life.

## THE DRAMATURGICAL PERSPECTIVE

*The Presentation of Self in Everyday Life* was first published by the University of Edinburgh in 1956 and later expanded for a second edition published simultaneously in Great Britain and the United States. The later version contains some cosmetic changes: it is divided into more paragraphs and the word "one" is substituted for "we"; but there are also important additions – a new section to the "Performances" chapter and an extension to the conclusion. Later I will suggest that these additions effectively overturn the book's main argument, and mark a central change of direction for Goffman's work as a whole. But for the moment I want to consider the common core to the two editions.

Goffman described *The Presentation of Self* as "a sort of handbook", a "report" outlining six dramaturgical "principles". These key terms generate an often bewildering array of definitions and classifications as they reorder the social world according to a theatrical perspective. The six principles are the performance, the team, the region, discrepant roles, communication out of character, and impression management.

Goffman defined a performance as "all the activity of a given participant on a given occasion that serves to influence in any way any of the other participants" (1959: 26). A few pages later he added: "I have been using the term 'performance' to refer to all the activity of an individual which occurs during a period marked by his continuous presence before a particular set of observers and which has some influence on the observers" (1959: 32). For performances to be successful individuals must demonstrate their conviction that what is enacted is "the real reality" while sustaining a viable "front", of stage props (such as desks for lawyers or white coats for doctors), appropriate facial expressions, and role attitudes (1959: 28). A person's front is a "set of abstract stereotyped expectations" that prepares audiences for the ensuing performance (1959: 37). Fronts add "dramatic realization" to performances: they help performers convey everything they wish to convey in any given interaction. For example, if a schoolboy wants to appear to be concentrating during class, he may lean forward and stare into the eyes of his teacher. The irony in this example is that the boy's theatrical efforts to appear to be concentrating are so consuming that he no longer has time to concentrate on the lesson. Dramatic realization highlights the distinction between something being the case and someone wanting something to be the case, revealing the difference between expression and action. Goffman exemplified this point by reminding us that the efforts of a Vogue model to appear cultivated are likely to leave little time for reading (1959: 42).

Performances are not only dramatically realized, they are also "idealized", that is to say, put in the best possible light and shown to be fully compatible with a culture's general norms and values. Whenever possible, we maintain expressive control of our actions so as to safeguard the fragile sense of worth. However, we also produce "negative idealizations" by putting our performances in the worst possible light. Panhandlers who feel that they will receive more money if they are thought to be completely removed from normal society are an example of this.

Performers are frequently obliged to misrepresent themselves. They do this whenever they make illegitimate claims. Misrepresentations are possible because status is often only supported symbolically. This flimsy evidence can be exploited by others, often very persuasively. For example, although members of the British aristocracy can prove their birthright if asked, typically a credible accent and front are convincing enough. Impostors therefore rarely need forged birth certificates. The results are disturbing: "The more closely the imposter's performance approximates to the real thing, the more intensely we may be threatened, for a competent performance by someone who proves to be an impostor may weaken in our minds the moral connection between legitimate authorization to play and the capacity to play it" (1959: 66–70).

The picture that emerges is this: performances are both realized and idealized as our all-too-human selves are transformed into socialized beings capable of expressive control. During a performance the individual's attributes may be stretched to the needs of the occasion and different audiences will be held in a greater or lesser degree of "mystification", thereby allowing the performer to maintain a distance from which to appear more interesting. In many cases, Goffman notes, the only mystery is that there is no mystery, the dramaturgical problem being to make sure that this fact is never disclosed (1959: 75–6).

Successful performances are usually staged not by individuals but by teams, who share both risk and discreditable information in a manner comparable to a secret society (1959: 75–6). Teams are run by Directors who forgo performing themselves to arbitrate in intra-team disputes and allocate parts (1959: 102–3). They perform in "front regions" – spaces from which they are seen by their different publics. In these settings they are likely to be polite and aware of standards of decorum. Teams rehearse, relax, and retreat to "back regions" – areas where front-region performances are "knowingly contradicted as a matter of course" (1959: 110–14). A "guarded passageway" connects front and back regions. The success of front-stage performances often demands an agreement between team and audience to treat the front stage as the only reality. Examples of this can be found in funeral parlors: "If the bereaved are to be given the illusion that the dead one is really asleep, then the undertaker must be able to keep the bereaved from the workroom where the corpses are drained, stuffed, and painted in preparation for their final performance" (1959: 116). There is extensive collusion here because at some point the bereaved must have met with the undertaker to discuss the details of the funeral and to establish a fee for these services.

Throughout his discussion of front and back stages, Goffman avoided the claim that authenticity can be regionalized; instead he suggested that context affects our perceptions of behavior in misinformed ways. Sometimes authenticity exists center-stage, sometimes it exists in a dimly lit corner.

The regionally variable behavior of team performances provides performers with secrets to keep. When knowledge of back-region activities is valuable, a variety of people with "discrepant roles" attempt to gain access by masquerading as team members. They aim to find out about the different types of secrets held by team members. Goffman distinguished five kinds of secret (1959: 141–3):

1 "dark secrets": facts incompatible with the team's image;
2 "strategic secrets": facts about what the team will do;
3 "inside secrets": facts which, if known, identify a person as a team member;
4 "entrusted secrets": facts which are kept as a demonstration of trustworthiness;
5 "free secrets": facts which can be disclosed without discrediting a team performance.

Various characters try to steal these secrets by gaining illicit access to the backstage. Each has a "discrepant role", such as informer, shill, spotter, shopper, mediator, non-person (such as servant), confidant, and colleague. Most have a right to backstage access that they abuse for their own gain. They can masquerade as a team member without being subject to the constraints that accompany team membership.

However, information can be gleaned from performances without individuals misrepresenting themselves: this occurs when performers disclose damaging facts inadvertently. They do so, as Goffman puts it, "out of character". Outbursts such as "Oh God!" unravel prior performances. These out-of-character outbursts take one of four forms. First, there is "treatment of the absent", which involves maligning the absent with either uncomplimentary role-playing or uncomplimentary terms of reference. Second, there is "staging talk" designed to assure everyone that all went well. Third is "team collusion" with part of an audience. Their selection holds them to a special relationship with the team. Finally, there are "realigning actions" where there is recourse to humor and comments such as "It was a joke".

The fear of disclosing discreditable information encourages performers to practice the art of "impression management" and to avoid unpleasant "scenes" in which each individual's projected self may become irreconcilable with a presented self (1959: 206). In these dreadful times an individual depends on the tact and charity of the audience to limit the extent of interactional damage. Audiences are tactfully tactful. Should their collective performance become strained or too self-evident then the "dramaturgical structure of social interaction is suddenly and poignantly laid bare" and outbursts of laughter or remonstration are necessary to cover the rapid realignment of teams and performers (1959: 227).

The overall tenor of *The Presentation of Self* is of a world in which people, whether individually or in groups, pursue their own ends in a cynical disregard for others. On the rare occasions when audience and performer cooperate, both endeavor to return hastily to the shelter of their various masks and disguises and avoid disclosing their inner selves. The view here is of the individual as a set of performance masks hiding a manipulative and cynical self. I call this the *two selves* thesis.

For the second edition of the book, Goffman chose to include some passages that threaten this characterization of self and metaphor, and it is to these passages that I now wish to turn.

## DISCREPANCIES BETWEEN EDITIONS

Both editions of *The Presentation of Self* outline six theatrical principles that can be used to interpret everyday behavior. An elaborate series of subclassifications and examples represent the person as a cynical manipulator of social encounters. The picture here is of an individual hiding behind a performance. Underpinning this account are the metaphor of the theater and the confidence trick, both skillfully interwoven in a masterful literary display. Nevertheless, a series of deft insertions to the second edition brings the appropriateness of this imagery into question.

Doubt begins near the beginning of the book: in the Introduction to the second, but not to the first, edition Goffman distinguishes impressions that individuals give from those that they give off. The key to this distinction is the intentions of the individual: impressions that are given are used "admittedly", those that are given off convey information inadvertently. At issue is the performer's awareness of the performance (1959: 14). Following through the implications of this distinction leads us to the next of Goffman's additions to the second edition of *The Presentation of Self*.

This can be shown by a closer look at the first dramaturgical principle: the "performance". This has seven distinct branches, the seventh of which is "mystification" – a term referring to the ways in which people ("actors") accentuate some aspects of their performance while concealing others (1959: 68). Goffman suggests that people do this to keep their audiences at a distance (the assumption is that distance will make them appear enticing and mysterious). He cites the advice given to the King of Norway: avoid familiarity with "the people" in case they are disappointed (1959: 68).

In this example the practice of mystification is a device used by the King of Norway: it is merely an appendage to him. By thinking of the self in this way dramaturgical analysis reduces the person to a manipulator behind changeable masks and facades. Earlier Goffman expresses exactly this thought when he comments that the apparent cynicism of professionals is "a means of insulating their inner selves" (1959: 31). This expression reveals his explicit or implicit willingness to distinguish two selves.

When *The Presentation of Self* was reissued in 1959,

Goffman reconsidered his earlier account of the self. For the most part he limited his revisions to stylistic changes and the amplification of the general theme. However, at two key points he appended sections that challenge the *two selves* thesis. In a very curious way these sections are neither introduced nor distinguished from the prior body of text. Instead a second Goffman "voice" intrudes in a quietly disruptive fashion. This appended section, called "Reality and contrivance," is entirely new. The first sentence of this section mentions our common-sense acceptance of a model of human behavior based on the confidence trick. The ensuing pages then question this assumption, leading up to an example that profoundly disturbs the account of self on which both editions are built. In almost anecdotal fashion he notes:

> And when we observe a young American middle-class girl playing dumb for the benefit of her boyfriend, we are ready to point to items of guile in her behavior. But like herself and her boyfriend, we accept as an unperformed fact that the performer is a young American middle-class girl. But surely here we neglect the greater part of the performance. (1959: 81)

It is immensely significant that this example is not in the earlier edition, and it is likely that his suggestion that "we" have neglected the greater part of the girl's performance signals his recognition that he had done so. Inserting this example discredits the *two selves* thesis by exposing the analytic limitations of a reliance on the existence of a hidden manipulator. Goffman's claim that the greater part of the girl's performance is not her guile and contrivance but her enactment of a young American middle-class girl opens up a much more complex analysis of the person, for which a dramaturgical analysis is unsatisfactory. The ramifications of American dating practices for accounts of self concerned him throughout the rewriting of *The Presentation of Self*. At the end of the chapter on impres-

sion management he appends a new section about the
dilemmas facing young American girls in the 1950s. Here
there is no longer any reference to their guile and contrivance, instead there is an acknowledgement that the custom
of "playing dumb" leads to "a special kind of alienation
from self and a special kind of wariness of others" (1959:
229). Goffman cites one American college girl saying that
although she does occasionally play dumb on dates, the
experience "leaves a bad taste" (1959: 229).

The two examples of the King of Norway and the young
American middle-class girl show why dramaturgical analysis is of limited use: for while it is reasonable to classify
the King's efforts to keep a distance from "the people" as a
performance, it is unreasonable to classify the girl's actions
in the same way. This is because the King can both stop
his performance and separate himself from it; the girl's
"performance" of young American middle-class girl cannot
be distinguished from her sense of herself. The girl displays
a multiplicity of selves which are neither appendages nor
masks. This invites a picture of the person as a composite
of multiple selves, each of which projects a set of claims.
Goffman's later work is very much concerned with this.
This change of direction reneges on the image of the
hidden manipulator.

The 1956 edition of *The Presentation of Self* ends with
a suitably cynical conclusion: "the very obligation and
profitability of appearing always in a steady moral light, of
being a socialized character, forces one to be the sort of
person who is practiced in the ways of the stage" (1956a:
162). Exactly the same sentence appears towards the end
of the second edition (1959: 244). In the first edition it
is the culmination of the study: the text ends with the
thought that moral character is just a staged achievement.
The second edition downplays this cynicism by conclud-
ing with a new section entitled "Staging and the Self"
(1959: 244–7). The first two pages of this section attempt
to reformulate the self by distinguishing self-as-performer
from self-as-character. The distinction is couched in hesita-

tion, moving uneasily between the self as a being with "fantasies and dreams" and the self as a "peg on which something of collaborative manufacture will be hung for a time" (1959: 245). This appended section, and with it the second edition, end with words of caution about the dramaturgical vocabulary. In the face of his growing dissatisfaction Goffman informed us that "the language and mask of the stage will be dropped" (1959: 246).

One of the key distinctions between the two editions is that while the first pursues the theater analogy optimistically, the additions to the second present the metaphor pessimistically, as a line of inquiry that has more or less run its course. I want to suggest that the atrophy of the trope occurs because theatrical interpretations posit a cynical account of the individual as possessor of two selves, one manipulative, one performative.

After the publication of the second edition of *The Presentation of Self* in 1959, Goffman abandoned the extended use of the theatrical metaphor as a description of social life. In the mid-sixties he wrote about the use of game metaphors or social life, but in such a way as to emphasize the heuristic rather than the descriptive strength of the approach. I consider this account in the next chapter. Goffman's self-criticism of his use of the dramaturgical perspective can be read into this new attitude to the game metaphor, but his explicit critique only surfaced as a subtext to the much later *Frame Analysis* (1974).

## Goffman's Criticisms of the Dramaturgical Perspective

Beneath Goffman's attempt to establish the conceptual basis to *Frame Analysis*, there is a subtextual critique of his earlier dramaturgical model. I want to unearth this critique and then use it to reconsider the strengths and vulnerabilities of the theatrical analogy.

Goffman held high hopes for *Frame Analysis*, a book with a ten-year gestation period and the trimmings (and quite possibly the content) of a *magnum opus*. In it he attempted to formalize our knowledge about the ways in which context structures our experiences in order to offer a substantive analysis of the claim that experience and understanding are context-dependent.

The criticisms of the dramaturgical model are signaled on the first page of *Frame Analysis*: "All the world is not a stage – certainly the theater isn't entirely. (Whether you organize a theater or an aircraft factory, you need to find places for cars to park and coats to be checked, and these had better be real places, which, incidentally, had better carry real insurance against theft)" (1974: 1).

This attempts to implode the theatrical analogy, to show that the theater analogy is not only an inadequate way of analyzing the world of our daily affairs, it is also an inadequate way of analyzing the world of the theater. The key to exploiting the analogy is to limit the definition of a performance. Goffman's initial formulation in *The Presentation of Self* doesn't allow a negative case: according to it we are acting all the time. Goffman wrote that "*all* the activity of a given participant" is an example of social acting (1959: 26, emphasis added). This definition effaces the literal absurdity of metaphor. In *Frame Analysis* he corrected this, redefining the term "performance" so as to limit its applicability. In so doing he tacitly acknowledges his earlier mistake:

A performance, in the restricted sense *in which I shall now use the term*, is that arrangement which transforms an individual into a stage performer, the latter, in turn, being an object that can be looked at in the round and at length without offense, and looked at for an engaging behavior, by persons in an "audience" role. (1974: 124, emphasis added)

In this passage he showed that he was quite conscious of the earlier difficulties of his definition of a performance. Goffman then distinguished different types of literal stage performances, these ranging from nightclub acts and assorted contests to lectures and talks. These cases suggest that performances vary with the varying degrees of commitment attached to them by their audiences. Nightclub acts are, in Goffman's word, "pure", that is to say, "no audience, no performance" (1974: 125); and during performances audiences are expected to be suitably engrossed in the proceedings. With lectures and talks impurities can be found, minds wander, and the performer can cease to be center-stage. Different problems arise when audiences are not at the performance, as is the case with radio shows (1974: 147–55). The key to these reformulations is the implied shift away from actual interaction to the frame in which the interaction is occurring. As Goffman says laconically, "the first issue is not interaction but frame" (1974: 127).

Tied to his new definition of a performance is a new definition of social acting. Goffman clarified matters by pointing to the "basic conceptual distinction" between performers and their characters, thereby allowing us to talk about, for example, John Gielgud taking the part of Hamlet. The version of this in everyday life is a remark about John Smith being a loyal friend, bad father, good plumber, etc., since here it seems that John Smith is playing the role of friend, father, or plumber. The differences between stage and everyday performances are instructive: John Smith playing friend, father, and plumber is a man with a personal identity and a biography, and it is far from clear what it could mean for him to stop "playing" these roles. When John Gielgud plays Hamlet, his identity and biography are different from those of this character, whom he stops playing when the curtain falls (1974: 128–9).

The now more clearly established literal absurdity of the theater metaphor can be used to draw our attention to the differences between face-to-face interaction in social life and on stage. This analytic work points to the importance of a variety of everyday conventions which must be flaunted on stage. For example: for an audience to follow a play it is usually necessary for actors to finish their lines; in daily life this is not the case, and interruptions are a normal part of the "multiple channeling" of interaction (1974: 139–40, 146). Similarly, body alignments differ radically in stage productions, where actors must align themselves not for the encounter but for the benefit of the audience (1974: 140). Tacit information must also be explicated on stage; in everyday life the silence about such information is part of the manufacture of intimacy – these are the "entrusted secrets" discussed in *The Presentation of Self* (1959: 141–43). On stage the "involvement contour" of participants is much flatter than it is off it, where audiences are not there for the sole purpose of entertainment or enlightenment (1974: 142–4).

Goffman's self-criticisms explore the ways in which the vulnerabilities of the theater analogy can be used to generate discoveries about everyday social organization. This resource was unavailable to him in *The Presentation of Self* which over-extended the analogy, mistaking the theatrical part of everyday life for the whole of everyday life. As Goffman himself puts it towards the end of the book, the self "is not an entity half-concealed behind events [the *two selves* thesis], but a changeable formula for managing oneself during them" (1974: 573).

## CRITICISMS OF THE DRAMATURGICAL PERSPECTIVE

Sheldon Messinger et al. (1962) offer a largely supportive critique of the "dramaturgic approach" which aims "to raise some questions" about its applicability to the analysis of everyday life. Their approach owes a lot to their recognition of the significance of Sammy Davis Jr.'s comment that stardom required him "to be on" almost perpetually (1962: 98–9). "Being on" refers to Davis's feeling that public recognition continually thrust him "on stage" and in front of an audience. He felt, in short, a more or less constant pressure to perform. In a brilliant shift of focus, Messinger et al. then turn to the case of the mentally ill. There too one can identify the experience of "being on stage" – although in other respects their plight is very different to that of the celebrity: faced with situations in which people around them (their audiences) view their characters as discredited, the mentally ill often feel obliged to put on a performance of normality. Both the celebrity and the mentally ill experience the pressure to perform as an unwelcome interruption to their normal lives – the clear implication is that ordinarily they experience day-to-day life nonperformatively (1962: 105). Where does this leave or lead the dramaturgical perspective? Messinger et al. draw the conclusion that despite not being a replica of an individual's own consciousness, the "life as theater" model is nevertheless heuristically valuable (1962: 105).

Alan Ryan (1978) notes that although Goffman warns us not to take the theatrical analysis too seriously, he doesn't answer the question "how seriously is too seriously?" (1978: 65). Ryan argues that a major drawback of Goffman's approach is that it says nothing about motivation and goal-oriented behavior (1978: 68) – a point made also be Giddens (1984). Ryan draws a useful distinction out of this, arguing that Goffman is either aiming to show how people manipulate "role distance" in order to slip out of their accredited performances, or he is aiming to show how people use performances as aesthetic recreations of them- selves (1978: 68).

Alaisdair MacIntyre views Goffman's account as effec- tively reducing or "liquidating" the individual into a set of roles, into a "peg" on which performances are hung (1969: 447–8, 1981: 30–1). The result is that Goffman could neither see the intimate connection between sociology and moral philosophy nor provide the moral critique which, for

MacIntyre, is the central task of the social sciences (1981: 109). For MacIntyre the "peg" analogy is the key to understanding the weaknesses of the dramaturgical perspective.

Richard Sennett offers a version of MacIntyre's critique when he complains in *The Fall of Public Man* that Goffman offers a picture of society in which "there are scenes but no plot" (1977: 36). This image is now often intimately connected with the critique of Foucault's inexplicable epistemic shifts. Although beyond the compass of this chapter, the comparison between Foucault and Goffman is indeed worth pursuing.

MacIntyre's argument is rather compressed. Recently it has been unpackaged by Thomas Miller (1984), who, in a forceful critique, argues that Goffman's "purely observational method" (1984: 146) draws him into making inadvertent claims about the intentions of actors which his analysis cannot substantiate. Further, Miller claims that Goffman's analysis breaks down because it cannot adequately limit the notion of "social acting" (1984: 141–63). Miller too bemoans the lack of moral comment in Goffman's work, its thin and cynical account of self and its capricious flirtations with the very different perspectives of cognitive psychology and functionalism.

Anderson and Sharrock (1982) and Watson (1987) draw an apparently unrelated conclusion; namely that Goffman's use of examples involves the imposition is a "unity of purpose" which highlights and hides disparate phenomena in a way supportive to the thrust of his prior analysis. The result is that awkward data are discarded or overlooked (Anderson and Sharrock (1982: 85). In a phrase used by Watson also (1987: 11), the "solution comes before the puzzle" (1982: 86). The tenor of this critique is made more generally by conversation analysts against Goffman: almost invariably they believe that his use of invented data is a major handicap for his research (the best statement of this is Schegloff, 1988).

The thrust of these critiques is that Goffman's dramaturgical perspective over-extends the notion of acting or performing, that it offers an inadequate account of the intentions of actors and that it imposes its solution onto the phenomena it purports to explain.

## CONCLUSIONS

What remains of the dramaturgical perspective? As a comprehensive account of everyday life, it is inadequate. This should be no surprise, since it is based on the metaphorical view that "social life is theater", which is and must be literally absurd. The reason why this inadequacy comes as a shock is that theatrical interpretations of everyday life are intuitively believable, and because of this the metaphor seems to lose its metaphoricity.

Nevertheless, it would be wrong to conclude from this that theatrical metaphors are useless, and that our intuitive beliefs are simply misguided. Clearly, there is some truth to the claims that we play roles, mystify our performances, take part in team behavior, distinguish spatially between front and back regions, and generally display great skill at impression management. The key issue concerns the adequacy or limits of this account.

Metaphors both illuminate and hide aspects of our behavior. The question is whether we have to accept them as a limitation or whether we can use them as a springboard for theorizing. Doing the former means that we have to trace out the various ways in the social world is theatrical; doing the latter means tracing out the ways in which the social world deviates from our theatrical expectations of it.

Part of Goffman's early work is an attempt to give credibility to the dramaturgical perspective. The aspect of the social world that this illuminates for him is the inherent cynicism accompanying our self-presentations. His recognition of the importance of ritual leads him to concerns which are hidden by the theatrical metaphor. Methodologically,

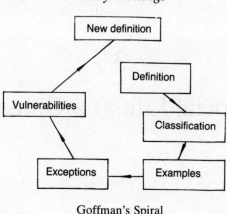

Goffman's Spiral

then, this suggests a "spiraling" strategy that explores the strengths and weaknesses of a variety of metaphors and perspectives. At one turn of the spiral he is close to the perspective, at the next its severest critic. This approach is not a resolution to the troublesome status of metaphor in sociological research but it is pragmatic. In his later work, Goffman usually treated the dramaturgical metaphor as an interesting stepping-stone to another analysis: a stop on the way rather than the final destination.

# 3

# Social Life as a Game

## INTRODUCTION

When we turn from the theater to the game metaphor a
similar set of methodological issues arises, but Goffman's
response to these issues becomes more explicit and direct:
at no point is there any doubt about the literal absurdity
of the metaphor. In *Encounters* (1961b) and *Strategic
Interaction* (1970) Goffman worked both with and against
the "grain" of the game metaphor. Working with the grain
promoted the view of social life as a calculative activity,
working against it promoted the importance of ritual.
Goffman's game analogy is, as we will see when we turn
to Thomas Schelling's work, not a reference to just any
game, but to a particular type of game. Schelling calls these
"mixed-motive games" and this describes very well the
paradoxical combination of manipulation and trust which
form the basis of our perhaps distinctively modern forms
of social interaction. Cities house not merely people but
strangers who together form a huge aggregate. As strangers
meet, they monitor and ratify each other with small but
endearing courtesies. Mixed-motive games are, then, the
smooth rails on which routine social interaction runs its
course.

Before turning directly to Schelling, I consider the attempt by Clifford Geertz to understand the significance of the game analogy in modern thought. Geertz ties his account to a particular reading of the analogy which is even more evident in Goffman's work than Geetz himself realizes. This complete, I will turn to Goffman's own appropriation of ideas from Durkheim's *Elementary Forms of the Religious Life*. Durkheim's explanation of the enduring significance of the soul provides Goffman with an account of what game-theoretic models hide from view. By then returning to Schelling I hope to prepare the ground for Goffman's formal specifications of the game metaphor. There is a curious similarity between the traditional "zero-sum" conflict games and the *two selves* thesis underpinning the dramaturgical perspective. But first an introduction to game metaphors in sociology.

## RITUALS AND GAMES

In an influential chapter, "Blurred Genres: The Refiguration Of Social Thought" (1983) Geertz argues that three decisive developments have altered the course and shape of the social sciences. They are: (1) that intellectual life has become increasingly accustomed to "genre mixing", with the result being that figures such as Habermas or Foucault slip between historical, sociological, philosophical, and literary pigeonholes; (2) that there has been a shift away from the search for generalizations and laws towards an approach based on "cases and interpretations"; and (3) that analogies from the humanities have become increasingly important, especially those of the drama, game, and text (1983: 19–35). Taken together, these produce the "refiguration of social thought" proclaimed in the paper's title.

The result has been that a "reductionist conception" of

the social sciences has been replaced by an emphasis on the "contrivances of cultural performance". Geertz suggests that "what the lever did for physics, the chess move promises to do for sociology" (1983: 22). Social theory has, he believes, become the domain of gamesters and people interested in aesthetics. Geertz expresses caution about this transformation, arguing that although analogical approaches to social-scientific problems are potentially enlightening, they also risk becoming little more than "elaborate chatter", playful talk about talk (1983: 23).

Geertz argues that Goffman is one of the leading exponents of this new style of social science, adding that his use of both game and theater analogies converge in the analysis of the social world as an "interaction game", as "ping-pong in masks" (1983: 24). Geertz's Goffman sees "gambits, ploys, bluffs, disguises, conspiracies and outright impostures" everywhere; everyone is playing enigmatic games whose structures are clear but whose point is obscure. Goffman's is a "play-it-as-it-lays ethic", a "bleakly knowing" and "radically unromantic vision" (1983: 25).

I think that Geertz's view of Goffman characterizes an element of his work very well, but that it misses his over-arching concern with the conditions of mutual trust which underpin our everyday experience of the world. It is in his discussion of a third analogy – the social world as text – that Geertz opens up the possibility of the reading of Goffman that I intend to pursue. Geertz suggests that a discursive view of everyday life raises the necessity of interpretation and of a conflict of interpretations. This idea is, of course, much indebted to Paul Ricoeur. Geertz closes the paper by warning that only the "wariest of wary reasonings" will be able to clarify the consequences and limitations of the drama, game, and text analogies for the interpretation of everyday life (1983: 35). Geertz's view of Goffman as a theorist of interactional manipulation must be offset by a view of him as a theorist of trust and social solidarity. For this it is necessary to turn from Geertz to Durkheim's analysis of the soul, one of Goffman's favorite pieces of sociology.

Durkheim's *Elementary Forms of the Religious Life* (1965) exercised an important but inconsistent influence over Goffman. Despite being generally ambivalent about Durkheim's methodology, rejecting both the function-alist concern with societal needs and the crude assertion throughout the book that Aboriginal culture is vastly simpler than French culture, he was nevertheless impressed by Durkheim's substantive analysis of the barely tangible threads which transform a mere aggregate of people into a society. Durkheim identified these threads by distinguishing the radically different roles of the magician and the priest: the former obtains a "sort of professional pleasure in profaning holy things", he established no lasting bonds, and serves not a cause but a clientele; the priest, by con-trast, solidifies a moral community amongst adherents to the faith (1965: 58–62).

The magician sides with the profane world, the priest with the sacred; this distinction runs through the book, defining both the nature of religion and of the individual's relationship to society. For just as the world is divided into the sacred and the profane, so too is each of us. "Man is double", Durkheim tells us, a profane individual and a sacred, social being (1965: 29). Our ethereal double enters and leaves us through any aperture, it is both part and not part of the body, it is, in a word, the soul (1965: 67). By a mysterious process, the profanity of the body is trans-formed into a sacred being (1965: 77). In a contradictory way, the sacred and the profane coexist together and apart.

Religions and societies comprise beliefs and rites. The simplest society, Durkheim claims, is the "clan" and its "cults". The clan and its beliefs are represented by a totem: an "emblem, a veritable coat of arms" (1965: 134), shared by all the members of the clan and no one else (1965: 123). The totem is the device maintaining the distinction between the sacred and the profane; it allows the members of a society to "vibrate sympathetically", joined together in a common bond (1965: 175). The totem is a society's "flag", a visible and sacred mark of itself (1965: 236), the merest fragment of which "represents the fatherland" (1965: 262).

Durkheim argued that in demarcating the world of sacred objects the totem symbiotically fuses the religious and the societal: "if it [the totem] is at once the symbol of the god and of the society, is that not because the god and the society are only one? ... The god of the clan, the totemic principle, can therefore be nothing else than the clan itself, personified and represented to the imagination under the visible form of the animal or vegetable which serves as its totem" (1965: 236). The consequence is that society is given a "moral authority" (1965: 237), through the idealization of which it recreates itself (1965: 466).

The individual figures in this account because his or her soul constitutes a small part of the sacredness of society itself. Durkheim then argues that what is true of Aboriginal culture is true of our own: "Today, as formerly, the soul is what is best and most profound in ourselves, and the preeminent part of our being; yet it is also a passing guest which comes from the outside" (1965: 249). He continued by saying that the honor owed to the totem will also be owed to the bodies which carry it. This is the point Goffman picked up in both "Communication Conduct" and *Interaction Ritual*; in the former he tells us that the person must be seen as a "sacred object ... to be constantly honored" (1953b: 103), in the latter that "the rites performed to representations of the social collectivity will sometimes be performed to the individual himself" (1967: 47). By virtue of being part of a sacred body – a society – and not being just part of an undifferentiated aggregate, the individual is owed ritual honor and care. Recognizing this takes Goffman far from the view of the self as a game-theoretic manipulator. Instead, the individual emerges as both a calculative and a courteous being. The final part of this jigsaw is still missing, then. It is provided by Goffman's staunch supporter, Thomas Schelling, to whom I now turn.

Schelling's game-theoretic approach to an alarmingly wide range of social problems – from the nuclear deterrence to the management of domestic disagreements – has been tremendously influential since the publication of *The*

*Strategy of Conflict* in 1960. In the Preface he characterized the direction of his argument very neatly: "The philosophy of the book is that in the strategy of conflict there are enlightening similarities between, say, maneuvering in limited war and jockeying in a traffic jam, between deterring the Russians and deterring one's own children, or between the modern balance of terror and the ancient institution of hostages" (1960: v).

From this passage it is already possible to detect similarities between Schelling's and Goffman's styles of work: both strive to bring together apparently disparate phenomena in novel ways, using extraordinarily obscure sources of data. Nevertheless, it is still a little surprising to find Schelling discussing Goffman in the midst of an analysis of the conflict between the superpowers (1960: 116). Schelling realizes that Goffman's acute examination of "face-work" raises a similar set of analytic themes to those raised by game-theoretic experts in the field of International Relations. Through many examples, Schelling tells us, Goffman shows that even the quite ritual demands of etiquette contain a "rich game-theoretic content" (1960: 128). Schelling shows this by citing Goffman's discussion of the way street sellers present a public face which the pedestrians will discredit should they decide not to buy their goods. As a result pedestrians find themselves trapped into purchasing something by their own considerate desire to "save face" – even though the face in question is not their own (1960: 128).

Goffman's *Strategic Interaction* (1970) was the result of a year's sabbatical spent at Harvard with Schelling. When asked recently to contribute to the *Harvard Guide to Influential Books* (1986) by choosing the five books which have been most significant for him, Schelling included *Interaction Ritual* (1967), commenting that he had been "hooked" on Goffman for thirty years.

*The Strategy of Conflict* is a rich source of ideas about the ramifications of game analogies for the interpretation of social behavior. Here I have to limit the discussion to two questions: the classification of different types of game and the role of trust in game theory; both of which have important implications for Goffman's work.

Schelling distinguishes three main types of game: *zero-sum* games which are governed by "pure conflict" (1960: 88); *coordination* games where pure conflict is to everyone's disadvantage (1960: 67) and *mixed-motive* games where players must reconcile zero-sum ambitions with the possibility of cooperative gains (1960: 89). Chess is an example of a zero-sum game, charades of a coordination game and, I shall argue, everyday life of a mixed-motive game. Central to Schelling's view is the belief that while the focus of many game-theorists on zero-sum options "yielded important insights", the methodology of this approach is inadequate for the study of situations in which players shift between conflict and allegiance. Zero-sum games are, then, "a limiting case rather than a point of departure" (1960: 83); similarly with coordination games, in which "pure collaboration" takes place such that players win and lose together. What both games share with their more elaborate mixed-motive counterpart is the assumption that strategy involves reciprocal expectations as teams guide their conduct by anticipating and responding to their anticipations of the "moves" of other teams.

The coordination game is a very useful preliminary tool for the analysis of everyday life. Schelling suggests that some variant of it underlies institutional stability: coordination games point to the traditional sets of rules which people can expect to be conspicuous candidates for general adoption. They govern by general consent, the standard case being everyday courtesy: "The force of many rules of etiquette and social restraint . . . seems to depend on their having become 'solutions' to a coordination game: everyone expects everyone to to expect observance, so that non-observance carries the pain of conspicuousness" (1960: 91).

The coordination game proposes a tacit social contract in which players receive payoffs whenever their choices

intersect. In zero-sum games players must of absolute
necessity avoid a "meeting of minds", as this will reveal
vital strategic intentions which can then be exploited; in
coordination games the meeting of minds is the players'
prime objective, since mutual knowledge allows strategies
to be merged as both players pursue paths of mutual
interest (1960: 96).

The theory of mixed-motive games drags analysis into
murky waters: players often find themselves bargaining
for resources without knowing the value opposing players
attribute to them. The result is massive uncertainty of the
kind exploited by all good spy stories. The questions "who
wants what and why?" are veiled in mystery. The zero-sum
game is oblivious to communication: winning is an all-or-
nothing predicament such that the available resources
are the only decisive variable. By contrast, mixed-motive
games involve the players' shared appreciations, pre-
occupations, and openness to suggestion, as well as that of
available resources. Communication is central to this game,
whereas for zero-sum options it is not even a peripheral
consideration (1960: 114–15).

It is self-evident that for zero-sum games *trust* is a
suicidal strategy and that for coordination games it is a
prerequisite. The key question concerns its role when these
two approaches are combined and motives are mixed. In
everyday life it is clear that in our everyday dealings we
all display appreciable quantities of trust in people known
only by proximity. For example, a woman getting into an
elevator with two strangers exposes herself to some danger;
what justification for her trust in them could she have? In
zero-sum game-theoretical terms her display of trust seems
irrational, because if the two strangers were confident of
avoiding retribution it would be in their interests to steal
from her (1960: 134). Schelling suggests one reason why
theft would be irrational: namely, that the pair have an
interest in the tradition of trust which makes possible a long
sequence of future agreement (1960: 134–5).

Although this suggestion is somewhat vague, it contains the germ of truth that underlies Goffman's sensitive deployment of the game analogy, and with this his analysis of day-to-day life. Trust is a necessary condition for routine social life to be possible: without an implicit and unconsidered confidence that buildings are safe, that supermarket food is hygienically packaged, that traffic rules will be obeyed, that pedestrians travel the streets without malign intent, "normal" life would be transformed into unmanageable and shapeless mayhem. The key question is not, for example, why people allowed concentration camps to be built during the Second World War, nor why student protesters in the 1960s defiled administrators' offices, but rather why these events are so rare and why we find them so surprising. Schelling tells us that "hardly anything epitomizes strategic behavior in the mixed-motive game so much as the advantage of being able to adopt a mode of behavior that the other party will take for granted" (1960: 160). Goffman explores these advantages in some detail, providing a pivotal analysis of the role of trust in everyday life.

## GOFFMAN'S GAME ANALYSIS

In *Encounters* (1961b) the game analogy is viewed as a "starting point" (1961b: 19), as a way of displaying the structure of real-life situations, albeit in ways which contain "important limitations" (1961b: 32). Unlike the dramaturgical perspective, the game analogy is good at suggesting the fatefulness of everyday life: the notions of winning and losing are central to all but coordination games. Goffman picks up on this by considering the world of gambling and casinos in *Interaction Ritual* (1967). But the origins of the game analogy are to be found in "Communication Conduct in an Island Community" (1953b). Extensive fieldwork persuaded him that everyday interaction has all the makings of a zero-sum game: in the hotel and street, in formal and informal settings, he observed the islanders extracting information about each other while revealing as little as possible about themselves. In both apparently consequential and inconsequential exchanges knowledge is fought over as a scarce commodity. For example, when the young men of the island leave for protracted trips to the mainland, little emotion is publicly expressed and farewells are kept deliberately short and low key; similarly, when guests arrive for dinner the woman of the house ignores their explicit praise of the meal and watches instead to see how quickly they eat it. Although these two examples are substantively very different, they both point to the way information is routinely withheld and uncovered in practices which Goffman calls "gain strategies", and from which he generalizes to the practices of "Anglo-American" society as a whole.

Gain strategists appear to be constantly on the look-out for the weaknesses of others; they are empire-builders, no matter how small or fragile their empires. Goffman suggested that gain strategies are so common "that it is better to conceive of interaction not as a scene of harmony but as an arrangement for pursuing a cold war" (1953b: 40). It is a cold and not a declared war because some kind of working acceptance is sustained so that daily life can continue. This acceptance, Goffman says, is one of the few bases of "real consensus" (1953b: 40). Later, in similar vein, he argued that everyday interaction is played as a game of "concealment and search" (1953b: 84) where information is won or lost in zero-sum terms. But the thesis subsequently downplayed this argument by stressing its limitations. Gain strategies are, he says later, only *elements* of an information game which is itself only part of the way we conduct ourselves in face-to-face interaction. As suggested earlier, in broadening his view, Goffman moves outside the game metaphor to consider the "ritual management" of encounters, thereby demanding that individuals must not only be "accommodated" in ways comparable to cold-war situations, but also honored as "sacred objects" and treated with ritual care. The language here is deliberately Durkheimian; it points to the necessity of limiting zero-sum calculations in order to attend to ritual matters. The gain strategist can ignore this instruction and continue unabashed, but the ensuing victories will be Pyrrhic and inglorious (1953b: 103). This fact is itself interesting: in everyday life "winning" is not enough; victors also require the moral approval of the vanquished.

Goffman's later work quite explicitly uses the mixed-motive game analogy devised by Schelling, channeling it through casino games and the world of espionage. It is to the details of these accounts that I now wish to turn.

The acknowledgements to *Interaction Ritual* (1967) reveal that he was working on an ethnographic study of casino gambling in Las Vegas; and a footnote in *Strategic Interaction* tells us that he had completed the fieldwork (1970: 122). The findings of this research have never been published and only fragments of it are available, scattered through different essays. From personal recollections of him it is clear that he took the activities of gamblers to be an important source of data about face-to-face interaction in general, and it is unfortunate that the Las Vegas study is unavailable to us.

His use of the game analogy works in two directions: sometimes he focused on the "action" generated by casinos, sometimes on the variety of "moves" made by agents in various forms of undercover operation. The implication is always that parallels to the everyday world exist: thus the "Expression Games" essay ends with the suggestion that a single structure of contingencies "renders agents a little like us and all of us a little like agents" (1970: 81).

On several occasions there are attempts to promote a casino vocabulary for the analysis of everyday life: in "Where the Action Is" (1967) the skeletal terms of such a vocabulary are given. "Action" is linked to "chance-taking"; it takes place during "plays" in which possible outcomes are subject to chance. Players risk a stake in an attempt to win a prize (the payoff). The stake and the prize combine to form the pot. The odds on winning can be theoretical (mathematical) or true (given known biases). "Pay" is the size of the pot after the player's bet has been subtracted. The reward for winning the pot must offset the risk to the player's stake (1967: 149–51). Action begins with the bets being staked; the game is then played, outcomes are revealed, and money exchanged. In a gambling vocabulary: action is "squared off, determined, disclosed and settled" (1967: 154).

Goffman supplemented this vocabulary in *Strategic Interaction* with a discussion of the different types of "move" available to players in non-casino games where action will not pass from settlement to disclosure in a fleeting moment. These moves range from the "unwitting" and "naive" gestures unconsciously made by individuals, to "control" moves designed to have an effect on the play and "uncovering" moves which attempt to reveal control moves. In addition, "counter-uncovering" moves can be played.

As an example of the full gamut, consider James Bond's "cover" on a recent mission: his control move is to masquerade as a gay hairdresser in an expensive boutique. One of his clients makes an unwitting move by asking "have you ever lived in Hastings?"; this being, unbeknownst to her, a secret password. Bond makes a naive move by assuming her to be his local contact, but soon discovers this to be false. An enemy agent attempts an uncovering move by propositioning Bond, hoping that Bond will inadvertently undermine his cover by his response. Bond then plays a counter-uncovering move by humoring the enemy agent and then leaving with him for an afternoon of passion in a nearby hotel. Bond's skill here is not merely theatrical; he has had to distinguish the agent's uncovering move from an unwitting one, and for this he has no definite criterion of proof. One man's uncovering move might be another's spicy endearments. On missions, however,

Bond may feel caution demands that he act his role to the full.

One of the distinctions between casino and spy games is that only in the former are outcome and payoff likely to occur in the same strip of experience – this, of course, is an important part of their appeal (1967: 156). Casinos offer conclusive and neat action which is unmatched in either the everyday or the espionage world. The price of the casino's packaged action is more than the risk to a stake: gamblers are also limited with regard to the form and content of legitimate moves. Games such as blackjack are played according to a semiotic which minimizes the possibility of either cheating during the play or argument after it: players are actively discouraged from touching their cards, and can signal their game intentions to the dealer without verbal communication. In the everyday or espionage world matters are more complicated. To begin with there is the problem of the desired outcome: whereas blackjack specifies the optimal score, elsewhere desirable ends are multiple and difficult to discern. This is an "embarrassment" for those using the game analogy, because clearly different players have quite different feelings about the same outcome. The value of the bet is, then, more than the payoff. This suggests that a payoff can be a means to another end – a thought Goffman faces at the end of *Strategic Interaction* by acknowledging that his fictional hero, "Harry", might be prepared to "lose" certain games in order to win the war (1970: 145). Thus, although the players' moves are central to the game analogy, they are used in situations in which the definition of winning is uncertain.

Game analogies are also complicated by the term "player", a term that hides important differences between players, who may be pawns, and thus in some bodily danger, or tokens, mere expressions of positions. From the history of diplomacy we know that a player may be a nuncio, that is, someone who represents a party; or a procurator, someone who negotiates on someone else's behalf. These positions are combined in the modern role of ambassador. From the history of the modern casino we also know that some players are shills, that is, gamblers employed by the House to generate the conducive atmosphere of a busy and successful establishment. They play with borrowed chips and to no advantage, their role being simply to occupy table spaces which might otherwise be intimidating to newly arrived gamblers.

Thus, there are quite different sorts of players who seek a variety of outcomes in quite different ways (1970: 87–9). Goffman warned us that although all words are performatives of one kind or another, knowing the weight they carry requires a prior knowledge of the kind of player who utters them (1970: 136).

The "murky notion of utility", the possibility of a multiplicity of desired outcomes, and the varieties of player point to the existence of important factors that are extrinsic to the game in progress. More than winning, players seek action, they want to know where it is and how they can get a "piece" of it. Action seekers stand in a curious position in relation to ritual: although often failing to pay ritual homage to those around them, they nevertheless uphold the principle of a ritual debt to the individual. The justification for their profanation of those obstructing their pursuit of action is that they are unworthy of ritual honor. Getting action allows the individual to display character and to evade routine; only those with similar ambitions are worthy of honor (however reluctantly given); everyone else has "bought in" to precisely those social arrangements that action seekers denounce. Gambling and chance-taking are used on such occasions as character displays of individual behavior; winning and losing are secondary considerations. In casinos, players seeking action use money as a "token" to be risked, elsewhere their bodies may be used instead, as in "games" in which players expose themselves to danger and physical pain.

Characters are built under the stress of situations governed by opportunity and risk; for the most part everyday life minimizes these. A developed character, then, demands the chance-taking action that routine social life is designed to avoid. Modern life, Goffman argued, lacks the fateful situations during which we affirm both to others and to ourselves our moral worthiness; in the absence of these situations we all express an ambivalence about "safe and momentless living" (1967: 260). Thus while some aspects of character can be easily affirmed, other aspects can be neither expressed nor earned safely. Careful, prudent persons must therefore forgo the opportunity to demonstrate certain prized attributes; after all, devices that render the individual's moments free from fatefulness also render them free from new information concerning him or her – free, in short, from significant expression. As a result, the prudent lose connection with some of the values of society, some of the very values that portray the person as he or she should be (1967: 260).

The game analogy conjures up the desire for a fateful life that is ill serviced by the vicarious and substitute experiences offered by television, films, and novels (1967: 262). Unlike these, casino games rejuvenate the self by manufacturing a manageable degree of instantaneous risk and opportunity, in the course of which player-heroes are treated as such by the House, which supplies them with the trimmings of luxury: expensive interiors, free food and drinks, and well-dressed and attractive attendants waiting to attend to any need (1967: 198).

The pathos of casino gambling is not the massive failure of an aggregate of players to beat the House (mathematics sees to that), nor is it the optimistic belief of some of them that they might; the sadness of the casino is found instead in the nickel-and-dime corners where individuals affirm a sense of self only to themselves and to a row of poker and blackjack machines:

> Commercialization, of course, brings the final mingling of
> fantasy and action. And it has an ecology. On the arcade
> strips of urban settlements . . . the customer can be the

star performer in gambles enlivened by being very slightly consequential. Here a person currently without social connections can insert coins in skill machines to demonstrate to the other machines that he has socially approved qualities of character. These naked little spasms of the self occur at the end of the world, but there at the end is action and character. (1967: 269–70)

The game analogy, then, points to the ways in which the individual can insert a "pull" against the world and thereby display character. By these means character itself is made; the self, as Goffman puts it, is "voluntarily subjected to re-creation" (1967: 237).

## CONCLUSIONS

Game analogies affirm fatefulness and character, they point to the calculative element in our everyday dealings and present us as information managers and gain strategists. Their limitation is that they obscure the importance of the ritual and trust which underpin our ability to carry on comfortably in daily encounters with a vast collection of people whom we know only through proximity. Goffman used the game analogy to show both these aspects of modern living.

# 4

# Trust and the Rules of Social Interaction

Trust . . . is a device for stabilizing interaction. To be able to trust another person is to be able to rely upon that person to produce a range of anticipated responses.

Anthony Giddens

## INTRODUCTION

In his early work Goffman considered both cynical and ritual accounts of everyday behavior. In the first edition of *The Presentation of Self* he emphasized the former at the expense of the latter. However, by the second edition of this book Goffman had decided that his dramaturgical emphasis on the cynicism of everyday performances was a mistake and that interpersonal conduct involved a strange mix of cynicism, ritual and trust. Goffman's view is that social life is what Schelling calls a "mixed-motive" rather than a "zero-sum" game.

This chapter looks at Goffman's analytic account of rules and his substantive analysis of their content. In the final chapter I will suggest that his work on rules is a preliminary statement that needs to be considered in the context of ethnomethodological findings.

## RULES IN SOCIAL LIFE

Let me begin with a condensed summary: Goffman characterized social rules as invisible, underlying *codes* governing our behavior. These codes are primarily constraints. Goffman distinguished substantive and ceremonial rules: the former are of importance in their own right, the latter not so. Most of his work focused on ceremonial rules. Rules simultaneously regulate and constitute the structure of social interaction, usually as background assumptions. Asymmetrical rules exercise power. Often rules surface as reciprocal obligations and expectations.

Goffman's most general pronouncements about the characteristics of rules suggest that they are analogous to traffic, grammar, or game rules; that is to say, they are external constraints. This Durkheimian view first appears in "Communication Conduct":

> Underlying each kind of social order we find a relevant set of social norms. . . . Norms, and the rules in which they are embodied, have a moral character; persons consider norms and rules to be desirable in their own right, to be binding in an obligatory way, and to be in some sense external to those who are guided by them. (1953b: 343)

In an essay published two years after his dissertation had been completed, Goffman provided a more explicit statement: "To study face-saving is to study the traffic rules of social interaction; one learns about the code the person adheres to" (1967: 12). In *Behavior in Public Places*, he once again describes the "social order" as a regulatory set of underlying norms which is akin to traffic rules (1963a: 8). The traffic-rules theme is used explicitly in *Relations in Public* to analyze individuals as "vehicular units" (1971: 26–40), where he argues that road-traffic rules serve as "something of an ideal case in arguments regarding the nature and value of ground rules" (1971: 27). Goffman's essay, "The Insanity of Place" (1969, repr. in *Relations in Public*, 1971), at about the same time draws out the family resemblance between traffic rules and grammar as under-lying codes. He argues that the interaction order obliges us to sustain "the grammaticality of activity", in contrast to the behavior of the mentally ill, which "strikes at the syntax of conduct" (1971: 424).

The first question mark against the view of social rules as underlying codes is raised in *Relations in Public*, where he says that "even quite formalized codes, such as the one regulating traffic on roads, leaves many matters tacit" (1971: 126). The recognition that even formal codes have tacit elements has important questions for the concept-ualization of what it is to follow and grasp a rule. However, the Presidential Address returns to the lexicon analogy: "The workings of the interaction order can easily be viewed as the consequences of systems of enabling conventions, in the sense of the ground rules for a game, the provisions of a traffic code or the syntax of a language" (1983b: 5).

Goffman saw these systems of enabling conventions as the consequences of a "consensual" and "contractual" order in which we all display our allegiance to a moral order and pay a small price for a large convenience. He admitted that this view is questionable but not that it is untenable (1983b: 6). He wrote here that "ground rules *inform* the interaction order" (my emphasis). What "inform" could mean remains problematic; perhaps a structuralism of sorts is at work.

Goffman assumed that social rules are an underlying code to human behavior. These rules can be understood in terms of a set of oppositions:

1 substantive and ceremonial rules;
2 symmetrical and asymmetrical rules;
3 regulative and constitutive rules.

In "The Nature of Deference and Demeanor" he described a *substantive* rule as "one which guides conduct in regard to matters felt to have significance in their own right" and a *ceremonial* rule as "one which guides conduct in matters felt to have secondary or even no significance in their own right" (1967: 53–4). Goffman's interest was mainly in this latter sort of rule, his aim being to show that the "gestures which we sometimes call empty are perhaps in fact the fullest of all" (1967: 91). Ceremonial rules are "sign vehicles" saturating the social world, sustaining or undermining what R. D. Laing calls an individual's "ontological security". The social fabric of trust between people is made up of these ceremonial threads. When taken separately they appear worthless; without them, however, our everyday surroundings – our *Umwelten* – are threatening and alienating (1971: 293–302).

Goffman distinguished two elements of ceremonial rules: deference and demeanor. The first refers to any sign of appreciation expressed through interpersonal ritual (1967: 55–7), the second to the individual's deportment – "what is required of an actor if he is to be transformed into someone who can be relied upon to maintain himself as an interactant" (1967: 77). Deference and demeanor coexist empirically and are only separable analytically. Deference should be distinguished from submission, because the latter is only the asymmetrical display of power (1967: 59). By contrast, reciprocal deference attests to "ideal guide lines" of conduct between people (1967: 60). I suspect that "people" here usually refers to strangers.

Deference itself is subdivided into "avoidance rituals" and "presentational rituals". The former protect what Simmel called the "ideal spheres" surrounding the individual. Avoidance rituals preserve a silence about embarrassing or discreditable episodes. They also preserve a silence about the preservation of silence. Presentational rituals are positive resources for honoring individuals. Goffman listed four: salutations, invitations, compliments, and minor services, and suggests that these attempt to persuade their recipients that they are not islands unto themselves (1967: 73). Presentational rituals provide a "symbolic tracing" of a normative order which is vital to the maintenance of trust in everyday life.

The second opposition distinguishes *symmetrical* and *asymmetrical* rules. Again, trust and power are at issue. The former describe rules involving reciprocal expectations, the latter those where no reciprocity exists. Common courtesies are typically reciprocal and symmetric, military salutes not so (1967: 52–3). The glaring exception is most gender rituals, in which asymmetrical rules are inverted as a theatrical way of emphasizing power relations. Thus, although women are, Goffman argued in "The Arrangement Between the Sexes", just another disadvantaged group, they are distinctive because they are held in high regard despite their disadvantage (1977: 307–9). In total institutions one can witness an analytically similar case when members of staff wait on inmates for the Christmas meal (1961a: 95).

Goffman also distinguished between *regulative* and *constitutive* rules, a distinction also used by John Searle (1969) to clarify speech-act theory. Regulative rules are of the form: "in these circumstances, do this", and are thus responses to context. By contrast, constitutive rules generate context. Nevertheless, Goffman thought that regulative and constitutive rules are empirically inseparable: "to describe the rules regulating a social interaction is to describe its structure" (1967: 144).

To sum up: Goffman demonstrated that social rules are not all of the same type: some are lexicon-like instructions, some are symmetric, some asymmetric, some surface as expectations, some as obligations. The most common form, however, is as a constraint on action. These constraints operate in the background of social interaction. Without these constraints the social world would be chaotic.

Although Goffman's analysis of types of rules reveals nothing of their content, it sensitizes us to the differences between different sorts of rules. The problem is that it exaggerates the extent to which rules are constraints. It is essential to see that only some rules in social life are comparable to the rules of games such as chess. In these games the rules are fixed and determinate: by contrast, rules in social life are indeterminate guides to the practical problems of daily social interaction. Tracing the differences between game rules and social rules is indeed instructive.

## RULES AS BACKGROUND ASSUMPTIONS

A recurrent problem in Goffman's work is the conflation of different levels of abstraction. His texts shift easily and smoothly from discussions of "Anglo-American society" to the recollection of something witnessed on a San Francisco sidewalk. The reader is left alone and largely unprepared for the task of piecing together the links between abstract pronouncements and concrete data. Goffman's persuasive examples inspire the belief that a bemusingly eclectic array of examples conform to an underlying pattern. In the preface to *Relations in Public* he acknowledged that his work lacks adequate "occurrence" and "distribution" qualifiers – difficulties exemplified by his frequent description of beliefs or practices as "ours" even though there is no obvious referent for this pronoun (1971: 18–20).

Rules are neither mere regularities nor are they laws. They are the practical knowledge of how to carry on; to follow a rule means to apply principles to circumstances in an indeterminate manner. There will never be a book for the rules of social life that is analogous to a book (the book) for the rules of chess, because it is impossible to specify all the contexts and all the possible "moves" open to interaction. As a result, for example, etiquette manuals can only list exemplary cases.

Goffman outlined the general principles to which we appeal in following everyday rules. At a great level of abstraction he claimed to have identified the constitutive rules which pervade every face-to-face interaction. These are not community bound, nor are they features of particular language games or forms of life. They are general guidelines about the kinds of things that happen during face-to-face interaction. Background assumptions are the "syntax" of everyday behavior, without which the "language" of behavior is incomprehensible. At times Goffman seemed confident that he had made material progress with the task of discovering these, at other times he made fun of his own "proclamatory excesses" (1981a: 1).

Goffman thought that social rules are largely constitutive of what we do when we carry on in a way of life: they form a deep structural code which generates an infinite variety of surface manifestations. They are embedded in what Giddens calls our "practical consciousness". We use them to make sense of the stream of face-to-face encounters. To understand a community, a lifeworld, a form of life, is in part to understand how perceived events correspond to this underlying code.

From his dissertation onwards, Goffman formulated and reformulated a small number of interactional principles that constrain face-to-face encounters. These principles loosely regulate interaction; they are schemata of interpretation. One of his most persistent beliefs is that for behavior to be construed as understandable – indeed, as sane – it must be generally acknowledged to have been derived from a set of interactional principles. Goffman referred to this demonstration of sanity as "Felicity's Condition". It is an assumption about our background assumptions.

Haphazardly and through many different books and papers, Goffman struggled to specify these interactional principles or background assumptions. At no point are they stated as formally as I do now, although his final paper, "The Interaction Order" (1983b), is a truncated effort to do so.

I suggest that the following background assumptions can be discerned in his work:

1   interactants must display *situational propriety*;

2   interactants must gauge the appropriate level of *involvement* for an encounter;
3   interactants must be *accessible* to all ratified participants;
4   interactants must display *civil inattention* in the presence of strangers.

Collectively, these constitute the SIAC schema, although admittedly Goffman never used this acronym. SIAC is underwritten by "Felicity's Condition", a presupposition about our presuppositions. Our public lives, he claimed, are spent demonstrating the imaginative ways in which we can demonstrate allegiance to the SIAC schema while sustaining a distinctive sense of our own identity.

## Situational Propriety

The notion of situational propriety is one of Goffman's few ideas that postdates his dissertation, although even there the emphasis on the characteristics of "faulty people" prefigures this later analysis (1953b: 258–72). The study of situational propriety and impropriety stems instead from his ethnographic work at St Elizabeth's hospital. Situational propriety refers to the practical knowledge of how to carry on in social situations. This awareness includes an awareness of body posture, spatial arrangements, conversational courtesies, and etiquette. Any or all of these issues comes to light when someone fails to demonstrate this practical knowledge. On such occasions, we conspire to explain away the individual's mistakes with all manner of excuses – tiredness, clumsiness, etc. However, if these excuses are insufficient we tend to attribute mental illness: "Much psychotic behavior is, in the first instance, a failure to abide by rules established for the conduct of face-to-face interaction – rules established, that is, or at least enforced, by some evaluating, judging or policing group. Psychotic behavior is, in many instances, what might be called a situational impropriety" (1967: 141).

In this passage Goffman only appears to be expressing a view about the nature of psychosis; in fact he is only commenting on interpretations of psychosis. On some occasions the failure to abide by the rules of social inter- action is symptomatic of some kind of mental illness, on others it is not so. His point is that situational improprieties often replace rather than point to an analysis of an under- lying disorder. At their most general, improprieties are the reverse side of public order: they reveal by default the rules we follow in order to make public life possible. Improprieties are the opposite of the "fine mesh of obli- gations" that allow "the orderly traffic and co-mingling of participants" (1971: 415). Thus, in *Behavior in Public Places* we read:

> ...when persons are present to one another they can function not merely as physical instruments but also as communicative ones. This possibility, no less than the physical one, is fateful for everyone concerned and in every society appears to come under strict normative regulation, giving rise to a kind of communication traffic order... (Incidentally, it is in this aspect of public order that most symptoms of mental disorder seem to make themselves felt initially.) The rules pertaining to this area of conduct I shall call *situational proprieties*. (1963a: 23–4)

These are thoroughly contextual and so their appropriate- ness depends largely on circumstance. Familiarity with many routine situations can mislead us into thinking that our actions are not context dependent; but this error is easily corrected by replaying the same actions in different settings. Then we see that the "delusions of a private can be the rights of a general; the obscene invitations of a man to a strange girl can be the spicy endearments of a husband to his wife; the wariness of a paranoid is the warranted practice of thousands of undercover agents" (1971: 412).

The argument that many symptoms of mental illness are demonstrations of situationally inappropriate behavior appears to offer an explanation of the "magical" ability of some individuals to be crazy one day and sane the next, because their "spontaneous remission" correlates not to their physiological or neurological states but to their breaches of public order rules (1967: 140). However, it is important to remember that many breaches of public order are disreputable, annoying, criminal, and anti-social while nevertheless being understandable. A man in a side street urinating on a car is committing situationally inappropriate behavior; but his behavior is understandable, especially if it is 11.30 at night and the sidestreet is adjacent to a bar. These facts allow us to attach a significance to the situational impropriety. Should the man urinate on his living-room table while his friends are eating the breach is harder to understand, although even then understanding is possible (Bataille, 1982: 16).

These two breaches of public order seem to reveal a sharp distinction between symptomatic and non-symptomatic situational improprieties. However, in "Mental Symptoms and Public Order", Goffman argued instead that this "folk conceptual apparatus" is inadequate because "there is no consensus, except in extreme cases, as to which of the two slots to put a behavior into. Agreement typically comes after the fact, after the label 'mental illness' has been applied, or (in the other case) after its applicability has been fully discounted" (1967: 142). This argument is also to be found in *Asylums*, where he states that all communities – including those of the allegedly mentally ill – are understandable once one is able to carry on in their forms of life (1961a: 266). However, elsewhere Goffman used our folk-conceptual apparatus. In "The Insanity of Place" he considered the way in which the "havoc" caused by the situationally inappropriate behavior of the mentally ill drastically fails to support the "grammaticality of activity" (1971: 424). He wrote: "the issue here is not that the family finds that home life is made unpleasant by the sick person. Perhaps most home life is unpleasant. The issue is that meaningful existence is threatened" (1971: 423). This seems to be a rather different account. The common ground is that the causes of situational improprieties are very complicated. Goffman made the point nicely: even "a loosely defined social gathering is still a tight little room [with] more doors leading out of it and more psychologically normal reasons for stepping through them than are dreamt by those who are always loyal to situational society" (1963: 241). Faced with this, the insensitivity of psychiatric language only "provides the practitioner with a handful of thumbs" (1967: 138).

## INVOLVEMENT

Goffman's most succinct definition of involvement occurs in *Behavior in Public Places*: "Involvement refers to the capacity of an individual to give, or withhold from giving, his concerted attention to some activity at hand. . . . Involvement in an activity is taken to express the purpose or aim of the actor" (1963: 43). The idea stems from his dissertation, where he suggested that the issue of involvement is closely tied to the problem of *euphoria*, with the general sense of ease felt in an encounter (1953b: 243). To say that people are at ease is more complicated than saying that they are relaxed, which suggests a disaffiliation from context. For Goffman, euphoria and involvement occur when participants in an encounter display an appropriate level of engagement with and commitment to a social gathering, where the notion of "appropriate" is lodged in the practical ability of participants to carry on in a form of life and is thus context dependent. As a result, the matter is felt most acutely in formal gatherings – precisely where one is obliged not to be relaxed but to be alive to the needs of the occasion (1953b: 250). Involvement is most commonly endangered by either a too noticeably self-consciousness attitude or by a too noticeably calculative one, both of which reveal the individual to be observing rather than participating in the event (1953b: 251–7). This point is expanded in *Interaction Ritual*:

> The task of becoming spontaneously involved in something, when it is a duty to oneself or others to do so, is a ticklish thing, as we all know from experience with dull chores or threatening ones. The individual's actions must happen to satisfy his involvement obligations, but in a certain sense he cannot act *in order* to satisfy these obligations, for such an effort would require him to shift his attention from the topic of conversation to the problem of being spontaneously involved in it. (1967: 115)

To be successfully involved in a social gathering, individuals must avoid the unacceptable extremes of alienation and selflessness. Goffman lists four types of alienation: "external preoccupation", "self-consciousness", "interaction-consciousness", and "other-consciousness", all of which distract interactants from a particular interaction by bring "extrinsic" factors to bear upon it (1967: 117–25). Great effort is put into resisting alienation, however understandable alienation may be. For example, on Dixon, "tales are told of the composure that some seamen showed under [threat], behaving as participants in interaction and not merely as men with their lives to save" (1953b: 283). Yet the interactional risk of such behavior is that the individual appears as a selfless entity and hence in some way inhuman or characterless. Appropriate involvement must therefore also show a degree of self-possession. Consider his observations from Dixon again: "Whatever the occasion, it seemed that the individual felt strongly obliged to show that he was not fully constrained by the events at hand; that he had a self available for interaction that could not be overwhelmed . . . Instead of conveying merely an involvement in the proceedings, the participant conveyed a delicate balance between involvement and self-control" (1953b: 274).

It is indeed a delicate balance, and when lost the individual is in danger of "flooding out". In *Encounters* (1961b), Goffman analyzed this issue by showing that certain people – such as surgeons – must learn to avoid flood-outs at all costs (1961b: 50–1). The theme is also explored in *Frame Analysis* where involvement is viewed as a matter of frame maintenance (1974: 345).

Goffman distinguished "main" or "dominant" involvements from "side" or "subordinate" ones, the former being those "claims upon an individual the social occasion obliges him to recognize", the latter those "he is allowed to sustain only to a degree" and in a manner subservient to the main involvement (1963: 44). Typically, side involvements expand to fill the time unused by main involvements. For example, a woman may "doodle" or read a magazine while waiting to see a doctor as long as she stops as soon as the doctor becomes available. Main and side involvements would be inverted if the patient decided to finish the picture or article before filing into the doctor's office. Of course, it is both possible and common to pursue both types of involvement simultaneously: this is an important interactional feat which allows individuals to match their attention to the "involvement contour" demanded by the activity at hand. A man who continues to watch a televised darts contest while his lover whispers sweet nothings into his ear has failed to match his conduct to this contour, but so too has a woman who listens too carefully to small talk, as has a junior officer who decides to go down with the ship. Main and side involvements are important complimentary devices because they allow us to show that, despite being well-socialized members of groups, we still possess a certain autonomy and distance from them. This duality can be seen when John talks to Marsha while exchanging a knowing glance with his brother, or when we see Marsha biting her finger while listening to John.

Provisions for the demonstration of autonomy are built

into the structural arrangements of everyday life, and this is central to the elasticity of quite routine social situations. Its importance is such that it is defended by portable items which Goffman calls "involvement shields" (1963: 38–42) that allow appropriate levels of involvement to be fabricated on difficult occasions. For example, one reason commuters carry newspapers is so that they can avoid the involvement pressures of train carriages.

## ACCESSIBILITY AND CIVIL INATTENTION

In *Relations in Public*, Goffman tells us that normally social life involves "non-acquainteds offering each other civil inattention" (1971: 260). This refers to something more elaborate than reciprocal indifference. In *Behavior in Public Places* he suggested that civil inattention demonstrates that "one appreciates that the other is present (and that one admits openly to having seen him), while at the next moment withdrawing one's attention from him so as to express that one does not constitute a target of special curiosity or design" (1963: 84).

Civil inattention is our means of accommodating the overwhelming majority of people with whom we have some contact during routine, day-to-day activities and of whom we know nothing – except snippets gleaned from proximity. It displays a delicate balance between the recognition of those around us and a studied deference to them. We respect their right to unaccosted anonymity. Like so many of Goffman's ideas, civil inattention appears to be a trivial feature of everyday life until one imagines situations in which it is pointedly absent. An historical example of this is the "hate stares" directed at Negroes in the United States (1963: 83); another the habit of treating service personnel and occasionally children as if they were "non-people" and hence unworthy of ritual courtesy (1953b: 223, 1959:

151–3, 1964a: 84); another the glare of attention afforded disabled and stigmatized people in many public settings (1964a). In all these cases, the breakdown of civil inattention is, at best, "a general cause for mild alarm" (1971: 286) and at worst a signal of racial violence. Civil inattention is the ritual honor and deference owed to strangers; its existence generates a sense of shared social reality which, if flimsy, is nevertheless enduring. Without it the social world is no more than an aggregate of people.

The question of accessibility extends this analysis by considering the reasons and occasions sanctioning infringements to the rule of civil inattention. Goffman's findings on Dixon suggest that "salutations . . . confirm and symbolize certain kinds of access to all other islanders" (1953b: 183). Without a means of piercing the protective bubble to deference and discretion which surrounds each of us – Simmel's "ideal-spheres" – social interaction would break down. Clearly there are many situations demanding exchanges between strangers which are not engineered along the predictable tracks of business or service encounters. Indeed, the implication of a person's deferential footing is availability for exchanges with all ratified strangers. With it we acknowledge a small sense of social solidarity.

The minimal involvement required by individuals to fulfill accessibility rules is perhaps most evident in day-to-day pedestrian traffic. Here people co-mingle with complete strangers in elaborate, if contradictory, displays of courtesy and indifference. There is, of course, the danger that the ritual access we grant people will be exploited: we "entrust" communication opportunities to people in a way that leaves us vulnerable to unwanted attention (1953b: 275). Panhandlers and collectors for charities exploit this communicative channel, disrupting civil inattention and making people pay for a speedy return to their protective bubbles. Street performers of various kinds are one of the best sources of knowledge about the limits and elasticity of public order in different settings.

In social life there are information channels which work through appearance, visual regard, intensity of involvement, manner, etc., and these can be blocked or facilitated. Street performers, drunks, children, comics, and the mentally ill provide data about what happens when the "promissory, evidential character" of the social world is shown to be either vulnerable to misleading (1983a: 3).

Goffman took up these themes in his essay "Response Cries" in *Forms of Talk* (1981a). Choosing an apparently circuitous route he considered the reasons for the sanction against "self-talk": "Self-talk is taken to involve the talker in a situationally inappropriate way. Differently put, our self-talk – like other 'mental symptoms' – is a threat to intersubjectivity; it warns others that they might be wrong in assuming a jointly maintained base of ready mutual intelligibility among all persons present" (1981a: 85). People talking to themselves are inaccessible to those around them, their conduct is situationally inappropriate, as is their auto-involvement. Goffman argued that we are wrong to assume that self-talk is irrelevant and trivial. Self-talk is a highly significant form of communication: it is how we explain (often explain away) our misconduct to others. The recipient of self-talk is therefore not the sender but the audience that observed the misconduct.

Consider the case of "spill-cries" such as "*oops!*". This is heard when a man knocks a glass over and has to pick it up, or when a woman heading out of a museum inadvertently walks past the exit. Spill-cries occur when we have momentarily lost control of some feature of our world. Although outbursts such as *oops!* seem unnecessarily to draw attention to the person, they are used because the failing in question is quite minor, and it is this feature of the incident to which the person wishes to draw our attention. Spill-cries remind audiences that the failing is small, easily corrected and atypical behavior. In addition, by emphasizing the *oo* part of "*oops!*", it is normally possible to get back in control by the time the "*oops!*" is heard. In fact, the absence of a spill-cry in such cir-

cumstances is normally a sign that something in the encounter has gone badly and perhaps irreparably wrong
(1981a: 101–3).

Although self-talk is sometimes acceptable, silence is
"the norm and talk something for which warrant must be
present" (1981a: 120). A person emitting a spill-cry con-
tradicts this norm in order to confirm to all present that,
despite appearances, the error should not be taken to mean
that the individual is in some sense "defective". Talk of
this kind seeks to confirm that the normal interpretative
framework is still in operation. Self-talk appears to be
a trivial appendage to everyday-language use, of little
interest to linguists or social scientists; Goffman shows it to
be a vital corrective to slippages in social interaction.

## FELICITY'S CONDITION: A PRESUPPOSITION ABOUT PRESUPPOSITIONS

In 1983 Goffman published an extensive paper in the
*American Journal of Sociology* called "Felicity's Condition". The paper argues that although there are a great
many presuppositions facilitating everyday encounters,
there is one presupposition underpinning all other presuppositions. This is Felicity's Condition, which is met by
"any arrangement which leads us to judge an individual's
verbal acts to be not a manifestation of strangeness"
(1983a: 27). It can be seen whenever our complicated
network of background expectations about language and
social interaction is brought to light. Not to be competent
in these matters is to break Felicity's Condition. This
term is a play on an idea of the Oxford philosopher, John
Austin, who tried to specify the conditions that must be
fulfilled if what we say is going to be understandable to
other people:

1. There must exist an accepted conventional procedure having a certain conventional effect, that procedure to include the uttering of certain words by certain persons in certain circumstances; and further
2. the particular persons and circumstances in a given case must be appropriate for the invocation of the particular procedure invoked.
3. The procedure must be executed by all participants both correctly and
4. completely.
5. Where, as often, the procedure is designed for use by persons having certain thoughts or feelings, or for the inauguration of certain consequential conduct on the part of any participant, then a person participating in and so invoking the procedure must in fact have those thoughts or feelings, and the participants must intend so to conduct themselves; and further
6. must actually so conduct themselves subsequently. (Austin, 1976: 14–15)

Goffman's hope – his "call to arms" – was that acceptable usages of background expectations may be quite structured and so susceptible to detailed analysis. If so, it would become possible to gather knowledge about the organization of taken-for-granted practices, especially with regard to everyday talk. In an attempt to develop an understanding of taken-for-granted knowledge, he pursued two very broad questions. The first concerned the presuppositions that make utterances meaningful, the second the differences between what is said and what is meant (1983a: 25).

The basic unit of Goffman's analysis is the "utterance" (1983a: 8) which usually presupposes three things: a prior "text", various matters pertaining to the immediate context, and a database of cultural knowledge (1983a: 21). These factors intermix with the "system-constraints" of language (1981a). An utterance may be longer or shorter than both a sentence and what conversation analysts refer to as a "turn's talk".

Goffman analyzed the management of Felicity's Condition by considering different imaginary utterances between either two friends (John and Marsha) or between strangers. The distinction between talk among the acquainted and that among the unacquainted is "central" (1983a: 30). Apart from a chapter at the end of the third section of *Behavior in Public Places* (1963a), this is one of the few explicit signpostings of the importance of this distinction, a point adding force to Denzin's observation that "Goffman's world of study fundamentally constitutes interaction among the unacquainted, the stranger, and only infrequently the friend" (1970: 127).

Goffman considered the ways in which Felicity's Condition acts as a constraint on behavior between the unacquainted by considering a scenario in which a woman sees a man whom she saw the previous night at a cinema. Since he is a stranger, it is impossible for her to approach him and ask, "What did you think of the movie last night?" unless there has been some prior contact with him or unless unusual circumstances thrust them momentarily into a common social world (1983a: 30). As he argued in *Behavior in Public Places*, "as a general rule . . . acquainted persons in a social situation require a reason not to enter into a face engagement with each other, while unacquainted persons require a reason to do so" (1963a: 124). The divide between stranger and friend is important enough to social organization to explain why so much effort is invested in bridge-building.

Drawing on the research of one of his doctoral students, Helen Gardner, Goffman considered one bridge between strangers – the solicitation of "free supplies" – the time, the date, a match for a cigarette, etc. (1983a: 37). Like panhandling, this form of soliciting exploits the fact that although there is a general rule against talking to strangers, there is a counterbalancing rule against showing a distaste for human contact (1983a: 35). In another paper, "The Arrangement Between the Sexes" (1977), he considered the ways in which rules of courtesy between men and women can also be used to justify talk among strangers.

The general characteristic of the bridge between strangers is that the first speaker's utterance reaches the recipient's mind by way of an unthreatening laconic remark (1983a: 33–4). Inventing such remarks – and circumstances in which to house them – is the skill of every successful comedian, philanderer, disc jockey, and politician. In a memorable passage, Goffman suggested that there are always methods for strangers to obtain information from us: "conversationally speaking, we are all information storage drums, and for every possible interrogator, there will be an access sequence that allows entrée to the files" (1983a: 47). Talk among friends is rarely understandable to other people, who lack the information to decode the flow of elliptical utterances. Friends can decode them by referring to prior turns of talk, the jointly perceivable surroundings, shared knowledge brought to the encounter and a grasp of delicacy and politeness (1983a: 28).

Utterances must also comply with presuppositions about the organization of talk. Thus the use of anaphoric expressions which presuppose their antecedents (and presuppose also that their antecedents are recognizable as such) is not merely a right but an obligation. Someone who says "I went to a movie last night. I didn't like it" has successfully used an anaphoric expression; someone who says "I went to a movie last night, I didn't like the movie" hasn't, and is in danger of breaking Felicity's Condition. There are also constraints requiring talk to be conditionally relevant and sequentially understandable. Usually, the critical information for an understanding of a turn's talk is held in the prior turn. For example, the meaning of "Are the chickens ready to eat?" depends on whether the preceding turn's talk was "The asparagus is done" or "The cows have been fed" (1983a: 8). However, there are occasions when meaning depends not on prior but on next turn's talk, as shown by the etiquette of checking that the recipient of a phone call has the time to talk (1983a: 15). Another exception is the appeal to the conversation's topic as a means of disengaging from prior turn's talk without endangering Felicity's Condition. This works by shifting from what is "given" in talk to what is "recallable" (1983a: 13). Frame-breaks can be used, although these tend to require an explanatory or apologetic prior utterance.

Among the acquainted, opening turns at talk often follow a recognizable conversational structure of greetings, update questions and answers, initial topic statements, mentionables and reportables. However, this account is made more complicated by deictic references that firmly root meaning in time and space (1983a: 14–17). For example, to understand the meaning of, "Ya alright Harry?" we need to know that the speaker is the driver of a newspaper delivery truck and that the query concerns Harry's stock of remaining newspapers (1983a: 15).

The "Harry" example suggests that taken-for-granted knowledge may be too complicated to classify. Goffman noted pessimistically that the "class of facts . . . is so immense as not to have much value" (1983a: 19). One limit might be set by Sacks's notion of "membership categorization devices" such as "bikers" – a term that slices up tacit knowledge along subcultural lines; another limit might be set by identifying the "phases" or "orderings" of different activities – such as the organization of telephone talk, where, for example, the answer "hello" almost invariably indicates that the caller has got through to a private dwelling; another is the idea of predictable courses of action, as when the owner of a restaurant forestalls further questioning by answering the query "Do you take American Express?" with "No, we don"t accept credit cards but we do accept personal cheques." Another limit might be set by technical knowledge which identifies the interests of the hearer; another by the familiar association of some categories of talk with each other, so that, for example, a bored participant in a conversation can reply with a "Really?" and other feedback remarks while thinking about what to eat for lunch (1983a: 20–1).

Understanding conversations requires the maintenance

of Felicity's Condition, the shared understanding of the system-constraints of talk, the correct use of anaphora and deixis, prior turns of talk, knowledge of context, topic, ritual constraints, and shared, personal information. However, even when all these conditions are satisfied, there are still opportunities for slippage between what is said and what is meant. This is because talk is not only about the exchange of knowledge and the performance of acts; it is also a way of affirming relationships, and what organizes these also organizes talk (1983a: 42). Indeed, in one sense a relationship is "merely a provision for the use of cryptic expression" (1983a: 42), a "celebration of recipient design" as friends build up a large corpus of "known knowings" (1983a: 18). This suggests that participant ratification is central to the structure of social interaction.

## CONCLUSIONS

Face-to-face interaction is usually orderly, routine, and predictable. These qualities are maintained through background assumptions that inform people about the expected range of behavior in diverse social situations. I have referred to these as Goffman's SIAC schema. Background assumptions are themselves underwritten by the fundamental requirement to demonstrate the sanity behind our actions. This is Felicity's Condition. Untangling it requires an understanding of the complicated ways that taken-for-granted knowledge is used in social interaction. Goffman thought that it will be very difficult to devise a framework that can classify the types and uses of taken-for-granted knowledge, although he was confident that it is used quite differently among the acquainted and the unacquainted. Among the former it preserves intimacy, among the latter, trust.

# 5

# Goffman's Sociology of Deviance and Conformity

## INTRODUCTION

In chapter 4 I suggested that an important strand of Goffman's work after *The Presentation of Self* analyzed the background assumptions that sustain and reproduce trust among strangers. In urban environments face-to-face interaction could easily become a terrifying ordeal, experienced with trepidation if not actual terror. Much of Goffman's work explains why we don't go through life in a cold sweat, and why instead our mundane encounters follow predictable paths that sustain our sense of what the social world is "really" like.

Sociologists have often assumed that social order requires a consensus about appropriate rules for conduct. This has meant that the study of deviance, with its focus on occasions of rule-breaking in everyday life, has become a major area of specialization. For functionalists this has certainly been the case, since the value consensus that preserves system equilibrium could be potentially undermined by rule-breaking behavior. Societies are thus thought to "need" rule-following to avoid pathological degeneration. This explains why, for example, Talcott

Parsons's *The Social System* considers deviance at some length.

Both the motivation and the justification for a functionalist sociology of deviance are simple to establish. Fitting Goffman into this account is more difficult, however. His emphasis on the intentions, ambitions, and reflexive actions of individuals is largely incompatible with a focus on value consensus as a system requirement. This is because it is very difficult to analyze the requirements of a social system if its citizens are viewed as merely its supports. Whereas Goffman saw societies as aggregates of knowledgeable agents, functionalists have typically seen them as aggregates of well-socialized individuals who fulfill their "status-roles". If Goffman is a sociologist of deviance, then he looks to be at some distance from the functionalism that has largely inspired this disciplinary sub-specialty.

One solution to this difficulty is to see him as a symbolic interactionist whose interest is not in rule-breaking behavior but in the meanings which people attach to that behavior. However, this definition collapses the study of deviance into symbolic interactionism. As will become apparent later in this chapter, Goffman used a standard definition of "deviants" as rule-breakers, even though he didn't think that different groups of rule-breakers had enough in common to warrant a single label. His views on this issue are most forthright in the final chapter of *Stigma*. Goffman believed that the most pressing problem for sociologists interested in deviance was the categorization of different types of rule-breaking. Once devised, these categories could ultimately replace the field of deviance altogether. His own work proposes two categories: stigma and mental illness. Persons in both of these categories have trouble sustaining the predictability of everyday life, albeit for very different reasons. I turn to these now.

## STIGMA: RULE-BREAKING
## AND THE FEAR OF DISCLOSURE

Despite teaching courses about deviance at Berkeley in the 1960s, Goffman was deeply suspicious of the field. His principal criticism of the sociology of deviance was that there is little chance of ever finding a general theory of deviance, without which the study of deviance is no different from a broad concern with social problems.

For example, Goffman sometimes suggested that the sociology of deviance is best thought of as a category devised by sociologists to give sociologists things to do. He explained this in the following way:

> It is remarkable that those of us who live around the social sciences have so quickly become comfortable in using the term "deviant," as if those to whom the term is applied have enough in common so that significant things can be said about them as a whole. Just as there are iatrogenic disorders caused by the work that physicians do (which gives them more work to do), so there are categories of persons who are created by students of society, and then studied by them. (1964: 140)

Goffman does add, however, that although deviants have too little in common to warrant a special analysis, some groups of deviants may constitute meaningful subdivisions that are worth "cultivating" (1964: 141). One group worth cultivating contains individuals with stigmata, since their efforts to preserve "soiled identities" can produce valid and interesting generalizations.

From Goffman's discussion we can discern three issues about the study of deviance:

1   Although there may be a coherent general explanation of rule-following in everyday life (this to do with the maintenance of trust and the necessity of routine and predictability), there will probably have to be a variety of explanations of rule-breaking. The consequence is that the

sociology of deviance needs to be broken up into discrete investigations, concerning, for example, deviance among powerful groups, deviance as mental illness, etc. It is wrong to assume that these different issues must have something in common simply because in some sense they are all occasions of rule-breaking in modern societies. After the fragmentation of deviance there will be no need for the initial label.

2  The nature of rules in everyday life needs to be clarified. The different kinds of rules need to be considered (see chapter 4).

3  The behavior of individuals who fail to follow certain types of rules may have enough in common to merit discrete analysis. For example, *Stigma* is an attempt to analyze the behavior of individuals who have been or may be discredited by public disclosures.

*Stigma* was initially a set of lecture notes for Goffman's deviance class at Berkeley. The book has five chapters, the first four of which analyze the ways in which we control the circulation of discrediting information about ourselves. The fifth chapter challenges the coherence of the study of deviance as a meaningful subdivision of sociology.

A stigma is anything that discredits us, and we frequently interpret a stigma as a symptom of an underlying moral failing which can be deeply discrediting. Clearly, stigmata threaten presentations of self, and thus they have to be understood against the backdrop of rules about appropriate behavior. We are constantly aware that our identities are discreditable and may be discredited in the future, even if they have survived in the present (1964: 4). Goffman used this observation to prompt a distinction between a "virtual" and an "actual" social identity, where the former is assumed and unchallenged and the latter is demonstrated and proven (1964: 2). Although a stigma is usually thought to be a physical blemish, Goffman's approach allows a much wider analysis. Physical abnormalities (Goffman begins the book with an excerpt from a poignant letter from a girl born without a nose) are only one type of stigma. As an example of another, consider the plight of some professional managers, for whom the lack of a college education may be a stigma that threatens their virtual identity, even though this supposed failing is not observable. It is worth noting here that a stigma does not necessarily carry the same meaning for everyone: in the above example, the failure of a professional manager to obtain a degree is a stigma; for a professional criminal, however, the presence of one may be equally stigmatizing.

Goffman suggested that there are three distinct meanings to the word "identity". A "social identity" is based on relationships to other people. A "personal identity" is tied to the individual's personal biography. Finally, there is an "ego identity": this refers to a individual's subjective sense of himself or herself as a result of various experiences. Each of these identities can be jeopardized by stigmata that expose discrepancies between virtual and actual selves. In each case, a projected self is shown to be untenable and embarrassment ensues.

There are various ways to manage or hide stigmata, all of which involve the sensitive control of information. The simplest solution is concealment, as when a bald man wears a toupée, a short woman uses high heels, or a lonely widow carries self-composed letters from imaginary friends. Concealment is often a tacit acknowledgment that the stigma in question is as discrediting as is generally assumed. A second strategy involves the use of what spies as opposed to bar owners call a "cover". A cover is a way of passing in a community by acting in an expected way. A cover can be quite simple, as when William Whyte gained access to gambling rooms merely be claiming to "Doc's friend" in *Street Corner Society*. Alternatively, it can be fantastically elaborate, examples of which have been recently documented by Gary Marx's study (1988) of undercover police operations, some of which involved the police setting up extensive businesses as fronts for their agents. A related idea is that of "covering", a strategy pursued by friends of a person with a stigma. For example, a woman who is hard of hearing may rely on her husband to give her hints about what is being discussed at a dinner party (1964: 102–4). A third and very different strategy for managing a stigma is disclosure, achieved by either flaunting a symbol of the stigma or the stigma itself. As Goffman wryly notes, this transforms the stigmatized person from someone with difficult information to manage into someone with difficult situations to get through (1964: 100). The difference is between a person who is discreditable and one who is discredited.

When considering the management of stigma as a problem of "passing" in social situations, Goffman returns to many of the themes of *The Presentation of Self*. For example, if we re-read *Stigma* as an application of impression management, then it is easy to see passing as a "cynical" performance enacted by someone with no belief in the part being performed. Similarly, it is possible to see "covering" as an example of the team's management of "dark secrets" known only to themselves (Goffman, 1959).

In *Studies in Ethnomethodology* (1967) Garfinkel also made use of the idea of passing, but in a way that is explicitly critical of Goffman's assumption that passing is a form of impression management. While discussing the curious situation of Agnes, a person with both male and female sex characteristics, Garfinkel argued that it was only correct to say that she passed as a woman in her everyday life if her life was considered episode by episode. In one episode, she passes as a woman born with a penis, which she likens to a "wart"; in another, she passes as an honest and open interviewee who is trying to answer Garfinkel's questions as candidly as she can. In others, she passes as a typical woman with her boyfriend, as a shy woman with friends on the beach, and as a confidant and relaxed shopper when buying dresses for the first time. When taken individually, each of these episodes does seem to exemplify Goffman's ideas about passing and information control. However, Garfinkel argued that this approach oversimplifies the complexities of everyday behavior. Specifically, it overlooks "inner time", during which we plan, anticipate, and reconsider our performances (1967: 166-7). If this time is added to the analysis, then passing becomes a continually unfinished project: we can never pass, we can only continue to work at passing. This involves the constant and recurrent negotiation of our various performances. Garfinkel uses this revised version of passing to great effect in analyzing the behavior of Agnes, who constantly re-evaluates her efforts to pass as a woman. Agnes's skills at passing were greater than even Garfinkel had appreciated at first. Several years after the initial research, he discovered that she had successfully passed (i.e. lied) to both him and his medical colleagues at UCLA. It transpires that Agnes was not a girl born with a penis but a boy who had taken hormones during early adolescence. These hormones had produced secondary sex characteristics, such as breasts, and had made him convincingly female.

Extending Garfinkel's analysis of Agnes to Goffman's analysis of stigma is instructive: it implies that the control of information by both the discreditable and the discredited is not a discrete act but a continuous activity. Thus the idea that a person can successfully manage information about a stigma suggests an unobtainable degree of security: in reality, maintaining an unblemished personal image is a continually precarious and unending project.

## MENTAL ILLNESS: RULE-BREAKING AND THE FEAR OF INCOMPREHENSION

There is now an extensive literature about the sociology of mental illness which addresses a range of concerns: historical conceptions of insanity (Ignatieff, 1978; Foucault, 1965; Scull, 1984; Rothman, 1971) the social conditions of psychiatric hospitals (Goffman, 1961a; Estroff, 1981), the role of socioeconomic and insurance companies in supposedly medical diagnoses (Conrad, 1980), the stigma associated with psychiatric labels (Rosenhan, 1973), and many others. However, one very basic question is central to sociological investigations of mental illness: what kind of phenomenon is mental illness? For many sociologists, the assumption held by physicians, psychiatrists, and the general public – that mental illness is a physical malfunctioning of the body – is precisely that: only an assumption. When being cautious, these sociologists publicly hold that there is simply insufficient evidence to define mental illness. However, when being less cautious, they suggest that the mentally ill are not physically ill at all, and that instead their "illness" is to break generally held rules of appropriate behavior. From this perspective, for example, the *Diagnostic and Statistical Manual* (*DSM*) used by psychiatrists is less a medical treatise and more a list of things not to be found doing in public. Clearly, the *DSM* is primarily a list of different kinds of behavior; the critical questions are (1) whether these lists are symptoms of underlying illnesses, and (2) the reasons supporting any claims that these underlying illnesses exist.

The iconoclastic psychiatrist, Thomas Szasz, is one of the few medical practitioners to suggest that mental illness may not be a physical illness at all, and may be instead a label for unusual behavior. Szasz summarized his views in this passage from his recent book, *The Untamed Tongue* (1990):

When a person fails to follow normal rules of conduct – that is, the rules most people follow – we say he is mentally ill, and when he does not respond to conventional rewards and punishments as we want him to respond – we say he is seriously mentally ill. It is true, of course, that one cannot treat many mentally ill persons "normally". But it is equally true that one cannot treat children, foreigners, the very old, the disabled, or the religious fanatic "normally" either. The reason is simply that insofar as people live by different rules, have different expectations, respond to different rewards and punishments, they will consider each other immature, strange, bizarre, or crazy – and difficult or impossible to live with. (Szasz 1990: 114)

This view is a concise summary of the findings of both the sociology of mental illness and of Goffman's own investigations. According to this largely sociological view, to say that a person is mentally ill is to speak metaphorically: it implies that because no one is really sure what mental illness is, the illness designation is only a temporary classification. Perhaps a great deal of the behavior that is now diagnosed as mental illness will one day be shown to be an illness with identifiable neurological and physiological characteristics; perhaps some of the behavior will be shown to be symptomatic of mental illness; perhaps only very little.

Goffman and Szasz are both very skeptical about the medical and scientific claims of psychiatrists. Goffman signaled this in the preface to *Asylums*, noting ironically that, unlike many patients, he began fieldwork "with no great respect for the discipline of psychiatry nor for agencies content with its current practice" (1961a: 8). At the end of the preface, however, he acknowledged that many psychiatrists had been fair-minded about his research. As evidence of the fair-mindedness of psychiatry, it is interesting to note that *Asylums* is now often referred to in psychiatry textbooks as an important study of the unintended consequences of the institutionalization of the mentally ill.

Szasz's mission is to make people aware of what he sees as the limited competence of the psychiatric profession. From his perspective, psychiatrists have failed to recognize that their claim that mental illness is a physical illness is a metaphorical and not a literal suggestion. The mistakes of the psychiatric profession derive from their failure to distinguish the metaphorical from the literal.

Goffman's mission was not specifically to debunk psychiatry: instead he wanted to use the findings of psychiatry in a new way. If Szasz is right to say that mental illness is about rule-breaking and not about physical abnormality, then the "antics" of the mentally ill should tell us a lot about normal, mundane, routine behavior. To put the matter crudely: Goffman thought that even though psychiatrists may not be very good at psychiatry, they may nevertheless be excellent sociologists. This is because psychiatrists have had to learn a sociological sensitivity concerning ordinary behavior; they have had to observe the behavior of normal people very carefully in order to distinguish it from the behavior of their patients. Goffman gave this view in the early paper, "Mental Symptoms and Public Order" (1964, reprinted in Goffman, 1967):

> Psychosis is something that can manifest itself to anyone in the patient's work place, in his neighborhood, and his household, and must be seen, initially at least, as an infraction of the social order that obtains in these places. The other side of the study of symptoms is the study of public order, the study of behavior in public and semipublic places. If you would learn about one side of this matter, you ought to study the other too. (1967: 139–40)

The implication of this argument, as Goffman notes, is that it should be possible to fabricate insanity, to "program" individuals to behave as if they were "crazy". This is because a convincing performance of craziness may not require destructive brain surgery, simply an incomprehensible attitude to the rules governing everyday behavior – break these and you risk people doubting your sanity. Much psychotic behavior is, Goffman believed, "a failure to abide by the rules established for the conduct of face-to-face interaction" (1967: 141). By extension, mental illness is, therefore, a collection of "situational improprieties", and insanity refers to a person's behavior and not to his or her bodily malfunctions. To understand this argument, it is useful to think about the following test: can psychiatrists identify mental illness in a dead body as easily as in a living one? According to Goffman (and Szasz), only then will they have demonstrated that mental illness literally exists, and is not simply a metaphor or label for unpleasant or unusual behavior.

In "The Insanity of Place" (1969), Goffman uses a very similar argument to analyze the interaction between people diagnosed as suffering mental illness and their families. The central claim of the paper is that both families and psychiatrists can be trapped in situations that force them to collude against the mentally ill patient, and that this collusion is extremely damaging. Patients suspect (often correctly) that their families and physicians are talking about them behind their backs. Goffman noted that then their suspicions tend to exacerbate their initial "symptomatic" behavior.

The unintended consequences of the decision to remove patients from the environments in which they are dysfunctional can also be dismal. The true price of psychiatric care may be very high: "dislocation from civil life, alienation from loved ones who arranged the commitment, mortification due to hospital regimentation and surveillance, permanent post-hospital stigmatization" (1971: 390). Goffman concludes that this is not merely a bad deal but a "grotesque one" and that patients recover in such circumstances in spite of the mental hospital, rather than because of it (1971: 390).

This is ironic because the group who is presumably the closest to the patient – his or her family – is also the one that is likely to make the initial contact with a psychiatrist or mental hospital. This is the first element that the patient perceives as betrayal. From then on many other betrayals follow. Patients realize that they are surrounded by "collusive nets" and "coalitions" that control perceptions of them by others. Patients begin to suspect, correctly, that their environment is being controlled in unseen ways. This control is either clandestine and totally concealed, or covert, when only the intent is concealed. In the first case, a family may close the door when talking to a psychiatrist, in the second, a family may tell their son that a psychiatrist

is treating "the whole family" while privately acknowledging that this is a sham, and that he is the only one
receiving treatment (1971: 392–3). This collusive practice,
Goffman claims, is actually a distorted version of everyday
behavior:

> A collusive conspiracy of course may be quite benign, may
> be in the best interests of the person conspired against.
> Collusion is a normal and no doubt desirable part of social
> life. Children are raised by it, especially handicapped
> children. Everywhere egos are preserved by it and faces
> saved by it. More important, it is probably impossible for
> interaction to continue among three persons for any length
> of time without collusion occurring, for the tacit betrayal of
> the third person is one of the main ways in which two
> persons express the specialness of their own relation to each
> other.
>    In ordinary medical practice, collusion is of no great
> issue . . . it is in psychiatric care that collusion becomes a
> questionable and troublesome business. (1971: 394)

This passage contains a double criticism of psychiatry,
suggesting that it is an unscientific manipulation of everyday skills and that it is harmful for the well-being of the
patients it tries to help.

What is mental illness? Goffman returns to this question
recurrently, examining and reexamining the idea that
mental illness is only a set of symptoms pointing not to an
underlying physical or neurological abnormality but to a
breakdown in our expectations for behavior in public
places:

> Mental symptoms, then, are neither something in them-
> selves nor whatever is so labeled; mental symptoms are acts
> by an individual that openly proclaim to others that he must
> have assumptions about himself which the relevant bit of
> social organization can neither allow him nor do much
> about.
>    It follows that if the patient persists in his symptomatic

> behavior, then he must create organizational havoc in the minds of members. . . . This havoc indicates that medical symptoms and mental symptoms are radically different in their social consequences and in their character. (1971: 412–3)

The havoc, we should infer, is not to do with faulty synaptic connections in the brain: rather it is something that undermines our basic adherence to SIAC and Felicity's Condition in public places, in bars, bookstores, and restaurants. Havoc occurs, then, because these background assumptions or rules about how people ought to act have been broken or ignored. It is important to be clear that Goffman does not think that mental illness produces havoc; instead he thinks (or at least suspects) that mental illness itself is this havoc. Phrased in this way, the hospitalization of the mentally ill takes on a new meaning: instead of being a curative institution, it now resembles a holding bay for individuals who are primarily a social nuisance. Goffman states this view elsewhere when he tells us that the "true clients" of mental institutions are "relatives, police and judges" for whom the behavior of the mentally ill is extremely disruptive (1961a: 334). These institutions may not be a haven for patients, but they ease face-to-face interaction for the rest of us.

Goffman's study of the culture of mental institutions, *Asylums* (1961a), is arguably his most controversial book. In four remarkable essays, Goffman describes the predictable pattern of day-to-day life experienced by patients in mental institutions. Although written in a "blankly neutral prose" (Ignatieff, 1983: 95) the book is a passionate and sensitive portrayal of people whose every movement is monitored and judged.

A couple of years after finishing graduate school at Chicago, Goffman obtained a grant from the National Institute of Mental Health to do research at St Elizabeth's hospital in Washington, DC. He began the project in 1955 when he and his wife moved to an apartment near the hospital (Winkin, 1988). Administrators at the hospital were aware of Goffman's research, and granted full access and a plausible role: assistant to the athletic director. This allowed him to roam wherever he pleased without drawing unnecessary attention to himself.

Goffman's findings offer a remarkable account of the social world of the mentally ill, and here I can only offer a cursory account of his detailed ethnography. In the first essay he described St Elizabeth's hospital as a "total institution", a closed environment in which the time and space of inmates can be controlled. Goffman claimed that the experiences of inmates in any total institution, whether it be a prison, monastery, military barracks, boarding school, or mental hospital, will be very similar (1961a: 16).

To summarize, life in a total institution has four distinctive elements:

1 all aspects of life are conducted under a single authority;
2 activities are conducted in the company of a batch of others, all of whom are treated alike;
3 there is a rigid timetable of events;
4 all activities are designed to fulfill the overall, official aims of the institution. (1961a: 5–6)

Upon entry inmates experience "civil death" and the "mortification of self": they lose their civilian clothes and rights, they have very limited privacy and they are forced to endure "batch living". Their personal territories are invaded and damaging personal information is publicly aired (1961a: 25–40). Inmates are "disinfected of identifications" and lose their "identity kits" (1961a: 28–9). The mortification of self is a profound attack on an individual's identity. Each inmate is removed, often abruptly, from a day-to-day environment that "confirmed a tolerable conception of self" and installed in an institution that crushes any sense of self-importance. In total institutions, presentations of self are precarious: there are few cosmetics or mirrors, clothes are typically provided by the institution and are dull and uniform. The result is that institutional life dramatically fails to corroborate an inmate's prior conception of self (1961a: 40). Even worse, inmates cannot escape mortifying situations, a problem Goffman calls "looping". In civil life, an embarrassed man can run out of the room, but in a total institution there is nowhere to run, and it is impossible for him to establish a distance between himself and a mortifying situation. Each activity is potentially a threatening attack on self as the dull domination of routine fills the inmate's day.

After this initiation is complete, total institutions attempt to rebuild their inmates" identities through the selective allocation of "privilege". Things that outside total institutions are easy to obtain are fought over inside them: cigarettes, toilet paper, coffee, access to television, etc. are given to inmates as rewards for good behavior. Goffman argued that the pettiness of privilege was as much a threat to a person's identity as the mortification of self. It is difficult for an inmate to sustain self-respect when he has had to act obediently in order to be able to receive, for example, a candy bar or a letter. In an effort to circumvent institutional rules inmates constantly look for an "angle" or a "gimmick" that will get them a desired commodity without antagonizing staff members.

In the face of the humiliating circumstances of privilege, inmates try to protect a sense of self by "playing it cool": they make a practical decision to make the best of dismal circumstances. Playing it cool involves four adaptation strategies: situational withdrawal, establishing an intransigent line, colonization, and conversion (1961a: 60–5). Situational withdrawal is a way of removing oneself from the total institution by daydreaming or fantasizing. Inmates lose interest in their immediate surroundings. One way of practicing situational withdrawal is to obtain newspaper accounts of baseball games and then relive them ball by ball. Establishing an intransigent line involves setting a lower limit to attacks on one's self identity, below which the inmate will resort to retaliation or non-compliance.

This can take many forms: inmates may barricade themselves in cells and smear the walls with excrement; alternatively they may go on hunger strikes. Colonization occurs when inmates make a favorable comparison between life in the total institution with life on the "outside", perhaps to the extent of planning ways to get readmitted when released. The fourth adaptive strategy is conversion: inmates give at least the appearance of accepting their superiors' definition of reality and themselves. Conversion is, perhaps, a cynical account of rehabilitation.

The irony is that these adaptations are both a rational attempt by inmates to preserve a sense of their own importance and acts that the hospital will interpret as symptomatic of mental illness. Goffman's argument is that the environmental attack on the self by a total institution has the unintended consequence of creating the symptoms it is designed to treat. Each strategy for playing it cool is likely to produce the situational improprieties that confirm the institution's initial diagnosis of each inmate.

Goffman also analyzed the staff world of the total institution, which he thought was caught in a constant tension "between what the institution does and what its officials must say it does" (1961a: 73). This tension is exemplified by the contrast between "people-work" and "object-work". When doing the former, staff maintain humane standards and attempt rehabilitation; when doing the latter they treat the mentally ill as if they were just objects to be "processed through an industrial plant" (1961a: 73). Staff members cannot reconcile the goals of control and therapy and end up confusing the two, as when they call solitary confinement "constructive meditation" (1961a: 82).

Clearly, there is the risk of violence as inmates resent the object-work performed by staff. Conflicts between inmates and staff are therefore minimized through a variety of institutional ceremonies that are meant to build solidarity. These range from in-house newspapers to slightly risqué Christmas parties in which inmates are given more leeway in their interactions with staff, shown perhaps through overfamiliarity during a dance or a skittish impersonation. The ability to tolerate these minor rebellions is a sign of the institution's strength, but also of its constantly precarious social reality (1961a: 92–103).

The second essay of *Asylums* introduces the idea of the "career" of the mentally ill. This describes the performance of any role over time. The concept contains no judgment as to the significance of the role in question. In this specific case, the role carries low status and is initially marked by feelings of embitterment and abandonment (1961a: 125). The career of an inmate has two stages: the prepatient and the inpatient phases. In the prepatient phase, individuals, often prompted by the doubts of others, begin to question their own sanity. In Goffman's terse phrase, there is a "disintegrative reevaluation" of self (1961a: 123). Various symptoms, such as talking to oneself or hearing voices, prove to the individual that he or she has failed to meet minimum stands of social competence. At this point, the person's world closes in around the definition of insanity. In these circumstances, admission to a psychiatric facility may bring welcome relief to the person, since at least this new environment is one with relatively few demands. However, Goffman warns that that the distinction between voluntary and compulsory admission is blurry. Indeed, for many prepatients, the various steps leading to admission were misinterpreted as general efforts by "friends" to solve their problems. In these circumstances, arrival at a psychiatric facility is a rude awakening to the true meaning of previous events and meetings.

Individuals are likely to feel betrayed by many people during the prepatient phase. Initially, their symptoms will have been identified not by a physician but by a friend, family member, or colleague. Thus, prepatients are usually betrayed first by someone close to them. These first doubts bring the prepatient into contact with a "circuit of agents" whose determinations can lead to institutionalization. This circuit of agents – social workers, psychiatrists, and lawyers – appears to be trying to help prepatients, but instead it deprives them of their liberty. Prepatients feel as if they have been passed through a "betrayal funnel". Even though they began with "at least a portion of the rights, liberties and satisfactions of the civilian", they end up on a "psychiatric ward stripped of almost everything" (1961a: 130).

Mental patients are caught in a "collusive net" of concerned friends and family who nevertheless "betray" them to the authorities (1971: 392). The result is a "career contingency": inpatient status in a psychiatric hospital. As in any total institution, inpatients experience a mortification of self. Prior conceptions of self are difficult to sustain, and the very people who appeared to be helping the patients are now the ones condemning them. Case notes are a good example of this process. Biographical information given freely by patients is subsequently used to confirm that they really are sick. Even when this information does not confirm psychiatric diagnoses, it can be written up in a way that casts doubt on the sanity of the patient. For example, Goffman reports that he read the following summary of a male patient: "No psychotic content could be elicited at this time" (1961a: 145). The implication is that although the patient is not showing signs of psychosis now, he will in the future. Phrased differently, the case summary could have said, "This man looks normal to me."

Institutionalization teaches inmates that "the self is not a fortress, but rather a small open city" that is easy to invade (1961a: 151–2). It teaches us that a person's self can only be sustained by confirmatory institutional arrangements (1961a: 154). Without such arrangements, we all begin to doubt our knowledge of who we are.

In the third essay Goffman closely examines the resources inmates use to survive institutionalization. These survival techniques are ways of "making out". By using them, inmates make their lives more tolerable while simultaneously affirming (to themselves at least) that they are more than the institution takes them to be. For example, inmates may find ways of stealing small quantities of coffee. This gives them both a personal supply of a scarce commodity and good evidence that they are not completely controlled by the institution.

The various strategies for making out are part of the "underlife" of any institution. They are more or less unseen by the staff, and if seen, they are tolerated to the extent that they do not challenge the smooth running of day-to-day life. They are necessary because a total institution exacts a high price from its inmates: "Built right into the social arrangements of an organization . . . is a thoroughly embracing conception of the member – and not merely a conception of him qua member, but behind this a conception of him qua human being" (1961a: 164).

Unlike accountants or lawyers, who are committed to roles that define what they do, the mentally ill are committed to roles that define who they are. As a result, the mentally ill are subjected to a "discipline of being" obligating them to act in certain ways. Goffman took this as a starting point of analysis and then proceeded to study the various ways that this discipline can be circumvented (1961a: 171). The initial imposition of institutional control requires inmates to make a "primary adjustment" bonding them to it. Later they make a "secondary adjustment" and learn how to get around the institution's assumptions about what they should do and hence what they should be (1961a: 172). Secondary adjustments preserve a fragile sense of self: they affirm that one person can stand against apparently overwhelming forces by developing an "underlife" of which the institution is largely unaware. Goffman put this succinctly: "whenever worlds are laid on, underlives develop" (1961a: 267).

There is an ecology to the underlife. Secondary adjustments typically happened in "free places" away from surveillance. The staff either don't know about their existence, or else they choose to stay away and relinquish a small part of their authority (1961a: 205). For the inmate, secondary adjustments affirm a sense of self and free places are a sanctuary from a threatening and restrictive environment. However, for the psychiatrist, secondary adjustments do not exist and free places are irrelevant. Instead, psychiatrists see secondary adjustments as either further symptoms of an underlying illness or as signs of recovery and convalescence (1961a: 186).

The fourth and last essay has a different focus to that of the other three. Instead of concentrating on the experiences of inmates in total institutions, this paper looks at the contradictory roles of the psychiatrist. In one sense, a psychiatrist is a professional like any other, with clients for whom he or she performs services. However, in another sense, a psychiatrist is more like a governor or officer who has an insidious institutional power (1961a: 308). This contradiction occurs because psychiatrists form a distinctive professional group. Professionals such as lawyers or accountants have clients with "malfunctioning objects", such as acrimonious legal settlements or messy tax forms. By contrast, psychiatrists have clients who are *themselves* the malfunctioning objects. It is therefore impossible for psychiatrists to separate clients from their problems, with the result that they "institutionalize a kind of grotesque of the service relationship" (1961a: 321).

## Criticisms of Goffman's Analysis of Mental Illness

There are a variety of substantive and methodological criticisms that can be made of Goffman's analysis. In this section I consider only the former, as the latter are addressed in chapter 7, in the context of a general analysis of Goffman's methods. Three principal criticisms can be made against Goffman's analysis of mental illness:

1 the medical model is much stronger than he suggests;

2 the notion of the "total institution" is vague;
3 the analysis makes no positive proposals.

Each of these deserves a word.

It is a mistake to assume that sociological and medical accounts of mental illness are indifferent to each other. Even though Goffman was critical of psychiatry, he clearly benefited from psychiatric efforts to categorize different types of behavior, since their work presents an extensive list of rule-breaking practices in modern societies. Medical practitioners can also make good use of Goffman's findings. As already noted, there is widespread acceptance of the general validity of Goffman's mortification-of-self thesis, and Goffman is frequently cited in relation to the dangers and unintended consequences of institutionalization. Goffman also alerts medical practitioners to the complexity of "normal" mundane everyday behavior. Particularly he draws attention to the importance of understanding the context or "frame" of everyday interaction. Without this knowledge, behavior is easy to misinterpret. Goffman is an important precursor of the very detailed studies of mundane interaction produced by ethnomethodologists and conversation analysts.

However, the most important contribution Goffman made was to provide psychiatrists with a benchmark against which to measure the validity of their studies. Goffman's analysis of conformity and deviance shows that symptoms alone are not satisfactory indicators of insanity; i.e. by staking out everyday behavior as distinctively sociological, Goffman forced medical practitioners to demonstrate the neurological, biological, or physiological bases of a genuinely *medical* account of behavior. In its strongest form, this leads to Szasz's demand that psychiatrists identify mental illnesses such as schizophrenia or psychosis in corpses as well as in living patients, since corpses cannot be diagnosed in terms of their unusual behavior.

A second and very different criticism concerns the usefulness of the concept of the total institution. Several writers, perhaps notably Perry (1974), Mouzelis (1971), Ignatieff (1983), and Davies (1989) have argued that Goffman either overextends the concept or leaves aspects of it vague. The key elements of Goffman's definition of the total institution are that (1) the inmates' time and space are controlled by a single authority; (2) the activities of inmates are conducted in large batches, and all inmates do the same things; (3) there is a detailed schedule of activities that is governed by formal rules; and (4) activities are intended to achieve institutional goals. Perry argued that many of these details are vague or subject to empirical variation. An example of vagueness concerns the second condition, for which Perry wonders how large a batch has to be in order to count as a large batch. Perry also shows that different examples of total institutions reveal very different forms of authority structures.

Mouzelis argues in a similar way, suggesting that Goffman's account of the total institution should be limited to formal organizations whose members (1) live and work on the premises, (2) did not choose membership, and (3) are stigmatized as a result of membership (1971: 118). Ignatieff supports this view, suggesting that the category of the total institution is "promiscuous at its edges" (1983: 95). He too suggests that the voluntary or involuntary nature of recruitment is a critical distinction.

Recently, Davies (1989) has presented a comprehensive review of the literature concerning the total institution. He shows that Goffman used the term loosely. In particular, Davies suggests that Goffman's analysis would have been clearer if he had referred to the total institution as a total organization. Explicit reference to total institutions as organizations clarifies three key variables: (1) the extent to which the organization controls the time and space of inmates; (2) the different formal justifications for total institutions; and (3) the different modes of eliciting compliance used by staff members in total institutions (1989: 83).

A consideration of these factors eliminates an assumption evident throughout *Asylums*, namely that life in a total institution is always a negative experience for inmates. Recent empirical research suggests that this assumption is false. For example, Davies cites Delaney's (1977) study of Buddhist monasteries in Thailand. Delaney discovered that although these organizations dominate the individuals within them, they do so in ways that can be both supportive and protective.

The third criticism of Goffman's sociological analysis of mental illness is that it offers no positive proposals for the treatment of the mentally ill. For example, among a barrage of sound and polemical criticisms against Goffman, Peter Sedgwick (1982) suggested that Goffman lacked the practical and historical knowledge necessary for an adequate understanding of the problems facing the mentally ill. The absence of in-depth understanding, Sedgwick argued, limited Goffman to shallow comments about situationally improper behavior that fail to recognize the complexity of mental disorders (1982: 48–51). These comments hide Goffman's conservative, functionalist, and largely amoral views about public institutions (1982: 62).

Sedgwick's key claim concerns situational improprieties; specifically, his claim is that this idea is too simple to explain mental illness. When put in this way, Sedgwick's argument has an intuitive force: most of us find it hard to believe that schizophrenics, manic depressives, psychotics, and others are perfectly healthy, "regular guys" who just break behavioral rules in public places. Instead it seems to be more plausible to say that they are ill, albeit in complicated ways.

At this point, it is essential to reiterate Goffman's basic argument: excluding odd moments of excess, he did not claim that mental illness is simply a set of situational improprieties. Instead Goffman only claimed that if psychiatrists can only recognize (i.e. diagnose) mental illness through situational improprieties, then they have not got any proof that the mentally ill are actually ill, since they haven't used any physical tests of abnormality. The only data psychiatrists have are sociological observations about rule-following in modern societies. Perhaps these observations will turn out to be symptoms of underlying illnesses, perhaps they won't.

Sedgwick is right to say that the policy implications of this argument are vague, and that skepticism about psychiatric evidence does not help the people psychiatrists presently try to help. To this Goffman might add, "but neither do psychiatrists", as he says at the beginning of most of his essays concerning mental illness.

Despite the negative implications of this argument, the policy implications of some of Goffman's arguments are very significant. For example, the mortification-of-self thesis is a profound challenge to the rehabilitative ambitions of psychiatric facilities, and part of the reason for a dramatic shift in the treatment of the mentally ill in the 1960s. Doubt about the success of hospital programs, concern about escalating costs, and increased political interest in mental health nurtured a movement to keep the mentally ill in communities. This program of "deinstitutionalization" or "decarceration" was supported by intellectuals suspicious of psychiatrists, conservatives trying to cut public spending, civil-liberty groups interested in protecting personal freedom, and the general public who had seen films such as Ken Kesey's *One Flew Over the Cuckoo's Nest*.

This is not the place to document the results of this program. Here I can only say that the situation of the mentally ill has not been improved by their return to the communities who were trying to get rid of them in the first place. As Scull (1984) notes, decarceration is now often a long word for malign neglect.

# 6

# Goffman's Later Work:
# Frame Analysis

## INTRODUCTION: FRAMES AND EVERYDAY LIFE

In order to understand Goffman's use of the word "frame",
it is useful to think about legal evidence and eyewitnesses.
Every day in court cases everywhere, eyewitnesses testify
about things they saw happen and their testimonies constitute legal evidence. Opposing lawyers have at least three
ways to challenge eyewitness testimony: they can undermine the credibility of the witness ("he was drunk at the
time"), they can question the possibility of the observation
("the street was poorly lit") or they can insist that the
witness merely interpreted observations that could be
interpreted quite differently ("the kiss was ritualistic not
sexual"). Goffman's interest in frames concerns issues
raised by this last sort of attack. He believed that our
observations are understandable only in terms of the frame
we put around them. Frames answer the question "What is
happening here?"; they tell us how to define the situations
in which we find ourselves. Frames provide a way of organizing our experiences. Without them, the social world is
only a chaotic abundance of facts.

Imaginative defense lawyers create frames at will which
show their clients to be innocent victims of a misunder-

standing or miscommunication. For example, when store detectives observe a woman slip two watches into her pocket and walk out of the building, she is transformed in their eyes into a shoplifter. However, a convincing lawyer can claim that the woman is not a criminal but merely absent-minded, and the two watches not contraband but presents for deserving nieces. The law encourages this defense strategy by requiring prosecution lawyers to demonstrate *mens rea* on the part of the accused; that is, it requires proof that the accused intended to commit a crime. From a legal perspective, then, the facts should not speak for themselves, and eyewitnesses and lawyers must elucidate the frames surrounding testimonies.

Clifford Geertz (1973) refers to a related issue as "thick description", an expression that has something in common with Goffman's "frame". Geertz draws on an old discussion by Gilbert Ryle about the difference between blinking and twitching to expose the perils of interpretation. Even though a blink and a twitch can presumably be physically identical, they are likely to be socially very different. Sociologists are thus exposed to the same interpretative dilemmas that beset us all. We see an incident but cannot decipher it until we install assumptions about what we are seeing.

In his major book, *Frame Analysis* (1974), Goffman tried to find out what these assumptions are and why we believe in them. He thought that if we can understand how these assumptions work, we will be able to show how the world "out there" is socially constructed. The image of the social world as a construction is very apt, because Goffman's frame analysis attempts to isolate the different elements of either the environment or behavior that convince us that what we see is genuine. As an example, consider male behavior at job interviews. Once the questioning and formal presentations are over, the interviewer may invite the candidate into his office, close the door, pour a couple of drinks, loosen his tie, and slouch in his chair. He may refer to the candidate by his first name and even offer a little personal information about himself. Each of these actions can be understood as an attempt to construct a situation in which the candidate can believe that the interview is over and that he is free to expose a self that he chose to hide during the ostensive interview process. Sitting with a loosened tie he can believe that what is presently happening is a post-interview ritual that is irrelevant to the interview process. Alternatively, he may believe that the "interview frame" is still operative, and that he is now experiencing an interview pursued by other means. And of course, how he chooses to act and what he chooses to say will depend very much on his reading of the frame. We could note that it will also depend on his degree of ingenuity, since the interviewer has provided him with an opportunity to "outframe the framer".

The underlying message of frame analysis is, then, that the procedures whereby we persuade others that what they see is real or genuine are precisely the same procedures whereby we cheat, deceive, or manipulate them.

Put in these terms, *Frame Analysis* appears to be a reworking of themes from *The Presentation of Self*, which showed people manipulating social situations in order to achieve certain goals. And it is true that both books show us how people manipulate our expectations. The principal difference is that *The Presentation of Self* is an extended metaphorical description of social life as a theatrical performance, whereas *Frame Analysis* analyzes the social world without relying on any particular metaphor. In parts of his early work, the dramaturgical metaphor was a guide to a new field of research, but later it became an unnecessary prop or even a hindrance that hid untheatrical but important aspects of everyday behavior. *Frame Analysis* can thus be thought of as a new edition of *The Presentation of Self* without a reliance on the dramaturgical metaphor.

*Frame Analysis* also has its roots in "Fun in Games", published in *Encounters* (1961b). This paper analyzes social life as a series of interactional "moves" between players, each designed to sustain a particular definition of the situation. Part of the skill of being, for example, a spy is to be able to identify aspects of either the immediate environment or a person's behavior that are incompatible with the prevailing definition of the situation. Spies employ an impressive practical awareness of framing matters. In *Frame Analysis*, we discover another group with comparable skills: "children who play doctor for naughty reasons are sustaining a [complicated] frame structure . . . The medicine that is practiced during this play is very childish, but the competency exhibited in regard to framing is already fully adult" (1974: 161, footnote).

Spies and children, then, both show that they are very aware of the gains to be made by manipulating framing assumptions. In *Frame Analysis*, however, Goffman traced his ideas not to his earlier books but to observations of otters at the Fleishacker Zoo in 1952, where Gregory Bateson realized that otters not only fight each other, but also play at fighting each other. This apparently simple observation opens up two important framing issues: (1) the behavior of the otters when fighting and playing at fighting is similar, but not identical; and (2) the otters are capable of transferring the meaning of one situation to another (Goffman, 1974: 40). If this is true for otters, then human behavior is likely to be subject to extraordinarily subtle frame manipulations.

In order to practice frame analysis, Goffman constructed a complicated analytic framework designed to identify the "lamination" of frames: that is, the superimposition of frames. Social interaction is often a composite of frames, each manipulating our understanding of the others. For example, the woman who strokes a colleague's thigh may do so knowing that both of them are happily married to other people and that the act will be interpreted as a friendly joke rather than as a sexual advance. But this meaning is only possible in the context of the frame that defines the situation as a routine day with routine banter in the office. But, of course, this "sexual pretense" lamination can itself be laminated with a frame with real sexual meaning, this one using the prior frame as subterfuge for an otherwise unacceptable communication.

*Frame Analysis* contains a framework and a very general discussion of these ideas. In later papers and in *Forms of Talk* (1981a), Goffman focused on empirical applications of frame analysis. After considering his framework and the criticisms thereof, I will turn to two particular investigations, the first concerning gender, the second disc jockeys.

## BASIC FRAME TERMS

Goffman defined "frame analysis" as an examination of "the organization of experience", and a "frame" as a principle of organization that defines a situation (1974: 11). Frames are used to analyze "strips": arbitrary slices cut from the stream of ongoing activity (1974: 10). Strips are the empirical materials subjected to frame analysis.

Social interaction is made meaningful by frames, the most fundamental of which Goffman calls "primary frameworks". To a greater or lesser degree, these organize our experiences into meaningful activities. There are two kinds of primary framework, a "natural" and a "social" framework. Natural frameworks define situations in terms of physical events that are unguided by human hands, such as the weather (1974: 22). By contrast, social frameworks make sense of events in terms of human intervention, and so reveal a concerned party guiding our understanding of a strip of interaction. For example, when Peter and Mary meet "by chance" in a coffee bar, both parties may interpret the event as one guided by the matchmaking hopes of a mutual friend. The framework of understanding is thus social. However, if they are unable to leave the coffee bar because of a thunderstorm, the framework becomes natural, since hope alone cannot bring about a felicitous downpour. In the first instance, then, understanding this strip requires knowledge about prevailing social frameworks; in the second, knowledge about natural ones.

Goffman argued that we become most aware of primary frameworks when our expectations about them are unhinged. He considered a variety of situations where this occurs. In the first, events occur which are so astounding that they cannot be accommodated within a conventional set of beliefs. Newspaper stories about Boston housewives meeting travelers from outer space or public displays of levitation are examples of this. A second challenge to primary frameworks is made by stunts, such as motorcyclists who jump across the Grand Canyon, magicians who memorize the names of entire audiences, and pinball wizards who play brilliantly even when blindfolded. In all three cases, the stunt lies outside our expectations and beliefs about what people can do. Primary frameworks are also brought into question by unexplained "muffings", as when the recipient of an award trips over the rostrum, and fortuitous happenings, such as a soldier being killed by a bullet fired at a funeral to commemorate the death of a comrade. Jokes and tense situations are a further source of trouble, since by their nature they undermine our sense of what is presently going on. Goffman discusses this in the light of several research papers about gynecological examinations, which show that a medical frame can easily be transformed into a sexual one (1974: 36).

Social life is, however, more complicated. Goffman suggests that any primary framework can be *keyed*. Primary frameworks are keyed whenever their meanings are transformed into something patterned on, but independent of, them. Bateson's observation of otters playing at fighting is a good example of a keying: the otters' behavior is patterned on a primary framework that defines the event as a fight, but this is transformed into a playful episode. Their behavior is meaningless to anyone failing to grasp the key. Goffman adds that close observation should reveal the ways in which participants are made aware of the keying, and also the cues which mark the beginning and end of the transformation.

If we think of a strip as a door, then there are clearly millions of doors and we might assume therefore millions of keys to "open" each of them. Goffman disagrees, however, arguing instead that there are only five basic keys to primary frameworks. These are: (1) make-believe; (2) contests; (3) ceremonials; (4) technical redoings; and (5) regroundings. None is self-explanatory.

A make-believe key playfully transforms a serious frame into a non-serious one. The keying is generally for the benefit of an audience, although an exception is day-dreaming, where the transformer and recipient are one and the same. Any kind of "dramatic scripting" is an example of a make-believe key: radio and television shows, theater and movie offerings, etc. Make-believe is only sustained by a considerable collective engrossment in the transformed frame, and as a result, spontaneous make-believe keys are likely to be short-lived.

The second key is the contest or game, which is loosely a keying of combat into a safer frame, although Goffman was unhappy about the generalizability of this definition to the many games which stress cooperation rather than conflict. Many children's games, for example, do not seem obviously combative (1974: 57). A contest may, therefore, have to be thought of as a key that maintains the drama of everyday life while transforming its consequential elements into inconsequential ones. For example, Robert Jackall (1988) has argued that American football is a game which re-plicates the perils of corporate life, with its leaders, fall guys, and go getters who "carry the ball" in dangerous situations. The difference is the degree of consequentiality: in football the game ends with a score rather than a dismissal.

The third key is the ceremony. Two categories of par-ticipants can be distinguished: the professional officiators and the officiated. The latter group use the ceremony to represent and epitomize themselves in one of their central roles, thereby temporarily transforming an element of their lives into the focus of them. For example, during weddings the role of spouse gains special mention for a moment, and the bride and bridegroom become principally, if not solely, identified with their roles for the duration of the service.

The fourth key is a "technical redoing". Goffman used this as an umbrella term for interaction involving rehearsals, demonstrations, exhibitions, practices, and role-playing. In all these cases, the here and now is transformed into a simulation of a real situation in the future, and is accompanied by the instruction to treat the frame as if it were what it purports to be. Exceptions to this rule occur when participants call a "time-out" to discuss appropriate responses, as when, presumably, the President stops a rehearsal of a news conference to ask his advisors how he ought to answer one of the questions they have just thrown at him. In the news conference itself such time-outs suggest incompetence rather than thoroughness.

The fifth key is the "regrounding". This refers to the substitution of one motive for another. Goffman gives the example of a "shill", a pseudo-gambler employed by the casino. Shills are employed for a variety of motives, one of which is to simulate action and excitement. Clearly, however, shills are not employed to gamble, even though their actions are designed to portray those of the gambler to other gamblers, who are thereby given company to lose in (1974: 76–7).

Also important is the fact that since a primary framework can be keyed, a keying of a primary framework can be *rekeyed*, and this rekeying transforms both the initial keying and the primary framework. Rekeyings can also be rekeyed in an infinite regress. An analysis of a strip of interaction must therefore "unpeel" the different laminations of a frame in order to discover its meaning or meanings. We might expect confusion on the part of the interactants as to which lamination they should be concerned with in order to sustain the interaction. The status of the interaction in the everyday world, on the other hand, is clearly determined by the outermost lamination or rim of the frame. For example, the outermost lamination of a frame of a play tells us that what is happening is make-believe, even though an inner lamination tells us, perhaps, that Romeo and Juliet are very much in love.

To recap: frame analysis analyzes strips of interaction to discover the underlying assumptions about what is happening in them. The basic frame is called a primary framework, which is either natural or social, depending on whether or not it is organized by human intervention. A primary framework can be keyed: that is, transformed into something patterned on but independent of it. A keying can be rekeyed: that is, transformed into something patterned on but independent of both the keying and the primary framework. A rekeying can itself be rekeyed in an infinite regress.

In addition to keyings, primary frameworks can be transformed by *fabrications*. A frame is fabricated when it is organized by a party in such a way that others will have false ideas about what is happening in the frame (1974: 83). The difference between a fabrication and a keying is that in the latter case everyone presumably interprets the frame in the same way, whereas in the former case one group is deliberately misled about the frame. Goffman identified two types of fabrication based on the ends each serves.

The first type of fabrication is benign because it is organized for the benefit of those it deceives. Benign fabrications are often thought to be morally justifiable, as in the case of a young musician who is misled to believe that his playing is pleasurable and not painful for his audience. The second type of fabrication is exploitative because it is organized for the benefit of the fabricator. The exploitation can be direct, as in a successful confidence trick, or indirect, as in the planting of discrediting evidence (1974: 87–109).

Keyings and fabrications undermine frames: they leave people unsure as to what is happening around them. Friends who joke around are amusing up to a point, after which their friends just want to know what they think. Similarly, the life of a spy is exciting in a movie but disturbing in reality, where every frame is potentially an exploitative and dangerous fabrication. Even though what is dangerous for the spy is likely to be only embarrassing for the rest of us, embarrassment is nevertheless good to avoid and it is reasonable to ask how we maintain trust in the sincerity or reality of everyday frames.

Goffman's answer to this was that trust in frames is maintained through the use of various procedures that anchor frame activity (1974: 247–51). This anchor ensures that the frame's purported meaning and its actual meaning remain identical. The fact that we almost always experience day-to-day life as a predictable and routine cycle of events is testimony to the heaviness of these anchors. It is psychotics and comics who cut the chord between anchor and frames, allowing them to drift in a sea of keyed and fabricated meanings.

Anchors use a series of devices to convince us that what appears to be real is real. Goffman outlined five of these: bracketing devices, roles, resource continuity, unconnectedness, and our assumptions about what we are all like.

Brackets tell us when a frame begins and ends and encourage us to respect the constraints they impose. They can be either external or internal. Brackets are external when they are not formally part of the activity, such as a school or theater bell summoning us to take our seats. Brackets are internal when they mark off a part of the ongoing frame as deserving a special and separate meaning. Internal brackets are, then, temporary time-outs (1974: 260). We frequently see both brackets at work; for example, professors use external brackets in order to call a class to order, and internal ones to tell them about their favorite movies. The former distinguish school activities from the lecture, the latter the lecture from chatter.

Social situations contain people playing roles which tell them and us what to expect in the ensuing activity. Frames are therefore anchored to the degree that the participants identify with the roles they play. In situations where participants take their roles very seriously, there is likely to be little doubt about the frame's meaning; in situations where the participants are easily visible behind their roles, there is likely to be some confusion about what is going on.

Activities are also anchored by resources that leave a residue that can later be traced. The fact that we can verify past events gives us reason to believe in them. Doubts about what really happened at, say, a banquet, can sometimes be quietened by gathering evidence. This approach works negatively by eliminating some explanations, and, like Sherlock Holmes, we are left hoping that only one explanation will remain when the dust clears.

The issue of unconnectedness is related to the gathering of evidence, because it is a reminder that many of the activities that take place within a frame are not relevant to our understanding of it. We anchor the frame, therefore, by not considering many of the things that are going on within it. Again, this can be considered in the context of espionage, since, unlike the rest of us, spies cannot assume that many background features of their environment are inconsequential. Instead, they must constantly investigate the frames in which they operate: for example, an open bathroom door may be unnoticeable to us but a cause of concern to them.

The final frame-anchoring device is an assumption we make about human beings: namely, that each of us possesses a single self that spans all the roles we perform. Beliefs about the constant nature of personal identity anchor a frame and limit its meaning. For example, if I fail to send a birthday card to my father, he interprets this as meaning that I am still as forgetful as ever; however, should my brother fail to send a card, my father would be worried that "something had happened", because he "never forgets" birthdays. In both cases, assumptions about the selves in question rule out some interpretations of the frame.

Up to this point I have suggested that frames are designed to organize the meanings we assign to strips of social interaction. This is true but incomplete: frames also organize *involvement*. In chapter 4 I devoted a section to an analysis of this term, and its significance in the SIAC schema. Summarizing briefly, the degree of involvement is the degree of commitment to a social encounter, and for each encounter there is an expected level of involvement. Goffman calls this an "involvement contour" and we all try to match it. In passing exchanges on corridors expected involvement is low, during lovemaking high.

In order to maintain involvement, interactants have to protect themselves from events that will cause them to "flood out". This is likely to occur whenever a person is observed in an act which is incompatible with his or her sense of self: composure is suddenly lost in laughter, embarrassment, or terror. Whichever, the frame will be lost. By contrast, there are also events which allow "flooding in" – the involvement of non-ratified participants in the frame. This occurs, when, for example, two friends loudly discuss football on a bus, thereby allowing other passengers to throw in opinions of their own. In these circumstances the initial frame is lost.

Goffman's empirical investigations of framing issues cast light on these dilemmas, and shortly I will turn to two very different examples, the first concerning gender, the second disc jockeys. However, first I want to mention some of the criticisms of *Frame Analysis*.

## CRITICISMS OF FRAME ANALYSIS

The reviews of *Frame Analysis* make three major criticisms: (1) Goffman's use of examples is misleading and tedious; (2) Goffman placed too much emphasis on the structure of situations and too little on the meanings people attach to their actions; and (3) the idea of a primary framework is underdeveloped.

*Frame Analysis* is a long book, long enough for some commentators to suspect that Goffman was being paid by the page (Davis, 1975). For Swanson (1975) and Sharrock (1976) the large number of examples makes for wearying and tedious reading, as each seems like "one damned fact after another" (Swanson, 1975: 219). The general consensus is that a good editor could have reduced the number of pages by 25 percent with no loss of meaning and a definite increase in reading pleasure.

It may be possible to correlate the length of the book with the length of time Goffman spent preparing it. However, it is more insightful to consider the role of examples in his overall argument. On the surface, Goffman used examples to help explain his various terms: frames, keys, fabrications, and so forth. At the same time, examples appear to confirm that the social world "out there" really is as the analysis represents it. To this extent, therefore, examples are not primarily clarifying devices; rather they are a (dubious) method of verification or confirmation. They give skeptics reasons to believe in the validity of the schemata. *Frame Analysis* is therefore a long book because the longer it is, the greater the apparent validity of its argument. Verhoeven (1985) makes a similar point:

> *Frame Analysis* can be characterized as an approach that is more interested in answering the questions of "how" and "what" rather than "why". Theory is reduced to generalizations that are formulated on the basis of a selection of illustrations. For the description of the different frames, a vast list of concepts is created, in which very often the personal motivation of the actor is considered. The fact-gathering is haphazard, which is justified by the structural interest. (1985: 97–8)

Unfortunately, the number of times a theory is confirmed is not always a good indicator of its truthfulness, and many false theories have been confirmed many times. However, if we broaden the idea of confirmation to include usefulness as well as truthfulness, then Goffman's inclusion of a large number of examples becomes understandable: examples emphasize the practical value of the theory itself. By the end of the book one is left with the feeling that even if there is a better vocabulary with which to analyze the organization of everyday experience, Goffman's is certainly very useful, and easily capable of considering a heterogeneous array of social situations. The reason, therefore, that *Frame Analysis* has so many examples may not have been primarily to clarify concepts or to offer insights about particular incidents in the social world, but to indicate the usefulness of its own schema (Jameson, 1976: 128).

Goffman's focus on frames has also been criticized for being more concerned with the classification of social situations than with the analysis of what these situations mean to the people experiencing them. This argument was made in a critical review of *Frame Analysis* by Denzin and Keller (1981), which had the distinction of being the only review of any of Goffman's books that received a reply. Goffman's comments are, to say the least, frosty; nevertheless, once de-clawed, their debate offers some interesting insights into interpretative problems in sociology.

It is quite clear that *Frame Analysis*, in keeping with his other books, attempts Simmel-like classifications of various social phenomena which are not detailed descriptions of particular strips of social interaction. Goffman himself described the early chapters as "stuffed with clumsy typologies and held together by string" (1981b: 68). The disagreement between Denzin and Keller and Goffman centered on the merits of these classifications. For the former, they were unnecessary abstractions that distracted attention from the lived experiences and processes through which meanings are created. For Goffman, however, the classifications presented in *Frame Analysis* outline the interactional devices people use in order to make sense of their lived experiences (1981b: 62). Therefore, an analysis of these devices is a necessary prerequisite to the more detailed research advocated by Denzin and Keller. Without it, sociologists would have to work on a case-by-case basis.

At the end of his reply Goffman made several self-criticisms, the most important of which was that he hadn't adequately developed the idea of a primary framework. *Frame Analysis* gives no indication of the range of possible primary frameworks. Unlike his analysis of the five basic keying transformations, his discussion of primary frameworks only distinguished the very general categories of the natural and the social. How many definitions of the situation can there be? What happens to Goffman's analysis if there are too many primary frameworks to classify? These questions are as yet unresolved. That said, let me turn to two of Goffman's applications of frame analysis.

## FRAMES AND GENDER

Patterns of inequality between men and women are often indexed by either resource allocation or career opportunities: a procedure which discovers that men typically have more of both. By contrast, Goffman did not index patterns of sexual inequality directly in terms of differential access to social structural rewards, but rather in terms of frame-analytic assumptions about the meaning of gendered interactions. Instead of documenting the "facts" of inequality – salary differences, promotion opportunities, etc. – Goffman investigated how men and women interpret their interaction. The ensuing analysis gives us a rather different view of social structure: it is now less a social fact (in the Durkheimian sense of an external constraint) and more a negotiated and hence challengeable joint accomplishment. Goffman's focus is thus on the reproduction of social structure in and through social interaction. How are women defined by men, and how does this affect interaction? And how, by extension, can these definitions be overturned?

However, caution is needed in assuming that inequalities between men and women can be understood as being primarily produced in social encounters. Much of this inequality is not an exclusive product of face-to-face inter-action, even though it is often most visible there. As Goffman put it, whether your job termination is handled abruptly or delicately, you've still lost your job (1979: 6). Nevertheless, sexual inequality is in part a product of frame assumptions, and it is these assumptions that Goffman wanted to analyze.

Goffman's analysis of gender is contained for the most part in *Gender Advertisements* (1979) and "The Arrange-ment Between the Sexes" (1977). He defined gender as any culturally established correlates of sex. These correlates can be observed in "social situations", which Goffman defined as arenas of mutual monitoring. In social situations we make "gender displays", which indicate our alignment to cultural definitions of sex differences, typically through a series of statement and reply couplets. Cultural definitions of sex differences are most explicit in "ceremonies", because these affirm basic social arrangements and present ultimate doctrines. They are also apparent in rituals, wherein we show respect for others in conventionalized and perfunctory ways (1979: 1–5).

For Goffman, ritual is essential because it maintains our confidence in basic social relationships. It provides others with opportunities to affirm the legitimacy of our position in the social structure while obliging us to do the same. Ritual is a placement mechanism in which, for the most part, social inferiors affirm the higher positions of their superiors. The degree of ritual in a society reflects the legitimacy of its social structure, because the ritual respect paid to individuals is also a sign of respect for the roles they occupy.

In *Gender Advertisements* Goffman hinted that it may be reasonable to trace the origins of ritual to military etiquette and court behavior, as deference is paid to royalty. These military or court frames are rekeyed in everyday life. For example, a military frame in which an enlisted soldier stands at attention and ends sentences with the word "Sir!" is now keyed into one in which inferiors call their superiors "Mr" or "Ms" and are called in reply "Frank" or "Suzie". Note that the meaning of the informality of the latter is no different from the meaning of the formality of the former, as both are concerned with who has control of whom. Other everyday rituals are subtle indications of the same thing. The suggestion that ritual in everyday life may be based on military etiquette is a fascinating idea.

Goffman analyzed three aspects of gender visible both in everyday life and in advertisements: (1) institutional reflexivity; (2) the parent–child keying; and (3) courtesy. He assumed that everyday rituals are a standardization, exaggeration, and simplification of everyday life, and that advertisements "hyper-ritualize" everyday life; that is, they standardize, exaggerate, and simplify everyday life even more dramatically than do everyday rituals. As such they are an excellent guide to contemporary gender relationships (1979: 84). His analysis is, then, a practical application of frame analysis.

Goffman referred to "institutional reflexivity" whenever an environment had been manipulated so that it exaggerated sex differences in order to justify gender inequalities (1977: 323). The term characterizes, therefore, any transformation of social relationships which intensifies the differences between men and women. For example, although it is a biological fact that women can and men can't breastfeed, it is a cultural fact that most societies have extended this difference to justify a sexual division of domestic labor. It is cultural because there is no obvious biological reason why women can and men can't wash dishes, clothes, or babies. Goffman notes that with only a "little organizing" industrial societies could be arranged so that biological differences had no appreciable consequences, but that instead there have been extensive

efforts to make biology more important than it needs to be
(1977: 301–2).

He considered five examples of institutional reflexivity:
the sex–class division of labor, siblings as socializers, toilet
practices, appearance and job selection, and identification
systems. Men learn that gender can be appealed to in the
face of unpleasant household duties; brothers and sisters
teach each other about their asymmetrical expectations;
segregated toilet arrangements provide backstage opportunities to affirm gender differences through same-sex
self-support groups; workplace arrangements encourage
women to obtain "meet the public" positions in which their
appearance justifies their paycheck (1977: 313–9). In each
of these cases, some aspect of biology is used to justify
some aspect of sexual inequality.

The parent–child keying interprets male–female rituals
as versions of parent–child rituals. Remember that Goffman
suggested at least once that some rituals can be traced to
military etiquette. This implies that gender rituals are a
keying of a keying. The first keying suggests that if the
world were in military uniform, then all adults would be its
officers, the second that men perceive that it is really only
the men who hold that rank (1979: 5). Gender relationships
are therefore defined as ones in which men should meet the
needs of women, protecting, indulging, and loving them as
a parent does a child. Women are also given license, indeed
they are expected, to flood out at emotional times, while
men stand stoically by their side. And by extension, all the
indignities experienced by children at the hands of adults
are likely to be re-experienced by women. Thus:

> . . . in our society whenever a male has dealings with a
> female or subordinate male (especially a younger one),
> some mitigation of potential distance, coercion, and hos-
> tility is quite likely to be induced by application of the
> parent–child complex. Which implies that, ritually speaking,
> females are equivalent to subordinate males and both are
> equivalent to children. Observe that however distasteful

and humiliating lessers may find these gentle prerogatives to be, they must give second thought to openly expressing displeasure, for whosoever extends benign concern is free to quickly change his tack and show the other side of his power. (1979: 5)

The third aspect of gender to be scrutinized was courtesy, which highlights a curious aspect of gender inequality. Goffman thought that although women are in one sense just one among many disadvantaged groups, they are distinctive because, unlike Black Americans or the physically handicapped, they are held in high regard despite their disadvantage (1977: 307–8). Courtesy maintains both the high regard and the disadvantage experienced by women. It is especially interesting because although it appears to oblige men to do certain things, such as raising their hats when coming into a woman's presence, this obligation is easily transformed into a selective license to harass women (1977: 312). Courtesy can thus be an exploitative fabrication. The muscular man who helps a petite women with her groceries appears to be altruistic, even though he may routinely ignore diminutive men equally overburdened outside supermarkets.

## FRAMES AND DISC JOCKEYS

In *Forms of Talk* (1981a) Goffman analyzed the experiences of disc jockeys (hereafter DJs) whose work requires them to project one, and only one, self during extended strips of "fresh talk": i.e. during extemporaneous talk (1981a: 146). DJs produce a fluent flow of words under conditions that lay speakers would be unable to manage, making remarkably few faults (1981a: 198). Nevertheless, they do make mistakes on occasion, and from one set of transcriptions Goffman classified and described different sorts of fault, distinguishing, for example, a stutter from a slip or a gaffe, and different corrective measures, these ranging from the truculent decision to "drive through" a speech error at one extreme, to the embarrassed "flood-out" at the other (1981a: 209–19). The professionalism of the DJ has made audiences more sensitive to on-air speech errors than to similar errors in everyday talk.

Speech faults are significant for DJs because they jeopardize their efforts to maintain a definition of the situation. A looser constraint affects lay speakers, although there are exceptions – as when it is felt that an individual should be upset, evidence for which should and is most easily provided by situated speech disturbances (1981a: 223). But such faults usually point to elements of a verbal performance that a speaker would prefer not to be identified with.

When DJs talk, they often manage to convey a sense of intimacy with people they cannot see and do not know. In the course of this they ritually honor strangers as if they were their friends. Goffman suggested that DJs do this by aligning themselves exclusively with what he called their *frame space*. The DJ's basic skill is the manipulation of frame space so as to project a universally friendly individual with a single self.

Fresh talk is the talk most easily understood and the one best exemplifying friendship, and DJs therefore try to simulate it, while avoiding the sensitivities of their audience. Thus, they steer clear of issues of race, religion, or political belief. Because of the heterogeneity of audiences there are all too many taboo subjects, each a possible cause of offense.

Goffman analyzed DJ talk by detailing their "footing" problems in situations where their erstwhile professionalism fails and they take a fall. This term refers to the participant's alignment and projected self during an interactional move (1981a: 128). When DJs make speech faults they lose their footing. Faults can be of this form: "To me English is an enema . . . enigma!" (1981a: 216). The projected self in this frame space is meant to be confident and friendly, but the DJ's anxiety leads to a loss of footing. DJs are also beset by "faultables": that is, by faults containing an ambiguity which would normally pass unnoticed in everyday talk. One of these is the "contextual unfreezing" of expressions, as when an ABC sports announcer declared: "Leo Lebel has been competing with a pulled stomach muscle, showing a lot of guts!" (1981a: 216).

Another faultable concerns problems of reference, shown by this newscaster: "The loot and the car were listed as stolen by the Los Angeles Police Department" (1981a: 245).

A different problem is that innocent words often carry salacious meanings, as in the following radio commercial: "Calling all parents, calling all kids! Here's your chance to buy a Davey Crockett bed – yes, friends, Hunt's Furniture Store has Davey Crockett beds – it's a twin size bed, just right for the kids – with scenes of Davey Crockett in action on the mattress!" (1981a: 252).

An odd exception is the Contestant show, in which presenters and participants alike aim to maximize faultables in the fault-free production of humor, but in general, avoidance is the norm. When faults do occur they can be left without a change of footing. However, should remedial work be attempted a delicate realignment will be required, as disowned selves must come to light. The most extreme case of realignment occurs when a DJ is party to an unmistakable disaster. In these terrible circumstances his final obligation is not to save face as DJ – that is already lost – but to save the self that is identified with what the DJ self has just said. The ritual talk which follows such disasters is a final honor to a fallen deity. Goffman found a beautiful example of this in the following commercial, in which a male announcer said:

Try this wonderful new bra . . . you'll especially love the softly lined cups that are so comfortable to wear. You gals who need a little something extra should try model 718. It's

lightly padded and I'm sure you'll love it. I do! . . . I mean
I like the looks of it . . . Well . . . what I am trying to say is
that I don't need one myself naturally, as a man . . . but
if you do, I recommend it . . . How do I know? I really
don't . . . I'm just reading the commercial for Mary
Patterson who is ill at home with a cold! (1981a: 302)

This segment of ritual talk highlights the distinction
between individual and self. The individual is "a palpable
thing of flesh and bone", a seeable entity. The self, by
contrast, is not a physical thing; instead it is a set of claims
made on behalf the individual. These two definitions allow
us to consider the different selves of the individual: on
some occasions these will be complementary, on others
contradictory or competing. We can understand the idea of
a person's footing as a projection of self which displays
a falsifiable claim about what the individual is. Ritual
talk endeavors to honor viable projections of self and to
accommodate discredited ones. In the above commercial
there is only one identifiable person, but there are many
selves that can be identified:

1  *listener's friend*: this self surfaces in the comment:
"You'll especially love the softly lined cups.";
2  *appreciative wearer of bras*: this fateful self emerges
in the line: "I'm sure you'll love it. I do!";
3  *admiring onlooker of bras*: shown by his statement:
"I like the looks of it.";
4  *self as man*: as in his claim: "I don't need one myself
naturally, as a man.";
5  *self as self-questioner*: the pertinent line is: "I recommend it . . . How do I know? I really don't.";
6  *DJ*: this is shown by: "Try this wonderful new bra.";
7  *self as human, all too human*: this appears in the
desperate comment: "I'm just reading the commercial for
Mary Patterson who is ill at home with a cold!".

This example provides data for what we all catch ourselves doing: changing footing so frequently that we fall
over. Ritual talk honors our successes and is tactful about
our failures. In the commercial, the announcer projected
contradictory selves in quick succession, only to find that he
had already discredited most of these by prior utterances.
Indeed, by the end the only selves that had survived his
*harakiri* were those concerning, first, his claim to be a man
and, secondly, his prosaic claim to be human, all too
human.

# 7

# Goffman's Methods

... traditional research designs have considerable limitations ... A sort of sympathetic magic seems to be involved,
the assumption being that if you go through the motions of
science then science will result. But it hasn't. (Five years after
publication, many of these efforts remind one of the experiments children perform with Gilbert sets: "Follow the instructions and you can be a real chemist, just like the picture on
the box.") ... Understanding of ordinary behavior has not
accumulated; distance has.

Erving Goffman

## INTRODUCTION

In this chapter I review three methods in Goffman's work:
(1) metaphor; (2) unsystematic observation; and (3)
systematic observation. I suggest that these methods are
designed to produce new ways of reordering familiar facts
and ever more general findings. The direction is from the
literary to the schematic: Goffman used various metaphors
and eclectic observations to chart an almost unexplored
area of investigation – face-to-face interaction. As he
became more confident of his findings, metaphors were
gradually replaced by formal definitions and classifications.

There is one point on which sociologists agree: Goffman was secretive about his methods. He rarely discussed methods of data collection and was willing to gather evidence from an eclectic array of sources, including newspapers, casual observations, and novels. As Graham Smith has written, Goffman was reticent about anything methodological (1989: 20).

Nevertheless, there is a precedent for Goffman's approach to sociology in the work of Georg Simmel, the brilliant and idiosyncratic German thinker. Simmel realized that everyday behavior was a subject matter for which he already had a vast supply of his own observations. Therefore, instead of producing survey or experimental findings that could be replicated, Simmel justified his work by claiming that critics could verify his arguments by their own observations. Simmel didn't try to discover new facts about the social world; instead he reordered old and previously disregarded facts. For example, consider his powerful description of the city as the site for the intensification of nervous stimuli, and his subsequent analysis of the blasé attitude that deadens this stimulation. In one sense, we already know this to be the case, in another it is a startling revelation.

Reading Goffman produces these same feelings. Although his methods appear to be only those of a sharp observer, his insights are undeniable. Goffman was certainly aware of the Simmelian quality of his work, commenting in the preface to *The Presentation of Self* that the justification for his work is the same as for Simmel's.

So, one method of inquiry, used by both Simmel and Goffman, is unsystematic, naturalistic observation. This research method amounts to reflections on eclectic observations. For many sociologists this is unacceptable and unscientific, a travesty of reliable research. Goffman himself commented that it has "serious limitations" (1971: 20). His defense was often to point out the weaknesses in other research methods. When feeling conciliatory, he suggested that sociologists should "keep faith with the spirit of natural science", even if this involves "kidding ourselves that our rut has a forward direction" (1983b: 2).

Although his own unsystematic observations were important, they were not his only method of gathering data. In addition, he also used participant observation, spending several years on three distinct projects, collecting data in a systematic way about crofters on an island off Scotland, inmates in a mental institution in Washington, DC, and croupiers in a Las Vegas casino. Until recently, little was known about how he did this work, but the publication of a talk he gave in 1974 (Goffman, 1989) has illuminated his ethnographic methods.

In addition to unsystematic and systematic observations of naturally occurring interaction, Goffman also used metaphor directly as a method of inquiry. The most well-known example of this is, of course, the dramaturgical model, discussed in chapter 2. However, he also made significant use of the metaphor that life is a game, discussed in chapter 3. For Goffman, metaphors were a way of testing out a new field of inquiry – they were preliminary ordering devices. In *The Presentation of Self* he referred to the dramaturgical metaphor as "scaffolds" which "should be erected with an eye to taking them down" (1959: 246).

## METAPHORS AS MODELS

Both sociologists and novelists investigate dilemmas of modern living, and it is possible to glean insights from, for example, Saul Bellow, Max Weber, Jacques Derrida, Virginia Woolf, and Erving Goffman, without worrying very much about which of them are or aren't sociologists. However, our expectations vary as we read sociology and literature: from the latter we expect an aesthetic sensitivity, while from the former an evidential sensitivity. Just as a badly written novel cannot be salvaged by being evidentially rich, so too a badly researched sociology paper is unlikely to be salvaged by a pleasant writing style. The distinction between aesthetics and evidence does therefore seem to be a good place to find an important difference between sociology and literature.

Sociologists want evidence that is valid and reliable. To get this they have methods which show that they really are measuring what they thought they were measuring, and results which skeptics can replicate. Traditionally, sociological research begins with the statement of a problem and then moves to a discussion of data collection. To the sociologist, an ingenious research design appears to be worth much more than an apt metaphor.

In his early work Goffman challenged this view by showing the importance of apt metaphors. He used metaphors as conceptual models rather than as words, exploiting our ability to extend their use to a multiplicity of settings. Metaphors can be "stretched" across many different examples. Thus, for example, his metaphor "life is a confidence trick" was shown to apply on all manner of occasions.

Understanding Goffman's use of metaphor requires an understanding of metaphor in general. In recent years the relevant literature has grown to an unmanageable size, and I cannot do justice to it here. My intention is simply to draw upon various studies in order to formalize a position which will assist a reading of this aspect of Goffman's work. Borrowing from Richard Brown's *A Poetic for Sociology*, I define metaphor in the following way:

1	metaphor involves the transfer of one term from one system or level of meaning to another; for example, Dante's "Hell is a lake of ice";
2	metaphor is literally absurd;
3	metaphors are meant to be understood;
4	metaphor is self-consciously "as if". (1977: 80–5)

When metaphors attend to fleeting resemblances between apparently disparate phenomena, they incite us to make a cognitive leap which then appears to be both inspired and self-evident. On such occasions metaphors seem to provide a link to an object's identity: they are ladders leading us to higher forms of understanding. But later still, these same metaphors can become disappointing, their resemblances unconvincing, their connections wearying, wrong, or patently absurd. Metaphor's nervous energy is then dissipated into loose formulations and its ladders are transformed back into snakes. More depressing still is the case of metaphors whose energy is not even dissipated but simply lost: they "die" and enter speech merely as literal expressions or as adjectives. "Skyscrapers" and "feeling lousy" are dead metaphors used now unthinkingly in everyday talk.

Any metaphor can be given up, allowed to perish, forgotten, or replaced by other metaphors; tropically speaking, change is the norm and permanence a masquerade. Advocates of this view hold to what Ricoeur (1986) calls a "substitution" theory of metaphor, which suggests that metaphor is no more than a concise way of expressing ideas.

A sizable body of work has taken a rather different view of the role of metaphor and other tropes in both the natural and social sciences. Instead of different metaphors exemplifying problems and solutions to questions in the natural and social sciences, these problems and solutions are themselves believed to be only examples of the influence of different metaphors. Not metaphor in the text of philosophy but philosophy in the text of metaphor, suggests Derrida at various points through "White Mythology", an essay in *Margins of Philosophy* (1982) that he acknowledges owes much to Borges's short story, "The Fearful Sphere of Pascal", which describes universal history as the study of the intonations of a few metaphors. Derrida and others regard metaphors as indispensable tools. With this in mind Richard Brown (1977) claims that the history of sociology could be rewritten as the investigation of the ramification of a handful of metaphors. This suggests that sociologists must adopt or be adopted by perspectives which then guide their view of the social world. Metaphor is not so much a word or a sentence as a conceptual system or model. Robin Williams puts this well when he says that "metaphor is perspectivism in miniature" (1983: 101).

This account of metaphor underpins *The Presentation of Self in Everyday Life*. Goffman's procedure here is, as several commentators have pointed out, remarkably like Kenneth Burke's "perspective by incongruity". Burke developed this idea through his attempt to pursue the implications of Nietzsche's "dart-like" style which works by its "constant juxtapositioning of incongruous words" (1965: 90). By doing this Nietzsche invented a variety of ways to order the everyday world. Similarly Goffman's *Presentation of Self* invented a vocabulary with which to consider anew what are otherwise quite banal daily events. With an array of apt redescriptions Goffman made the familiar, everyday world appear strange.

In *Permanence and Change* (1965) Burke argues that the Nietzschean idea of perspective by incongruity transforms the over-simplified classifications of sociological research into creative acts. However, he also warns that the "great danger" accompanying the use of any trope is that an insightful similarity can be mistaken as evidence of a shared identity (1965: 97). This danger is more evident in metaphor than in simile, because simile only states that, for example, love is "like" a red rose, whereas metaphor states that love "is" a red rose. The risk is that metaphor is transformed from being an insightful resemblance into an all-embracing world view. Perhaps metaphor is both a restriction and a deception; as Derrida puts it: metaphor "orients research and fixes results" (1978a: 17), a suggestion originating in Nietzsche's famous claim that truth is merely "a mobile army of metaphors". Linguists such as George Lakoff and Mark Johnson have pursued this line of enquiry, arguing that particular metaphors are entrenched in the way we think. For example, the metaphor "argument is war" structures many of our daily experiences, even though many of us would prefer to view argument in co-operative rather than military terms (Lakoff and Johnson, 1980: 3–13).

Goffman does use the theatrical metaphor to produce a world view, although he also questions the metaphor as well. I want to suggest that Goffman used metaphor as a way to explore a new area of sociology: the study of everyday life and face-to-face interaction. Metaphor served as a preliminary ordering device for this research. This characterization of metaphor has been made very eloquently by Quine. Consider the following passages: in the first Quine affirms the importance of metaphor for scientific research, but in the second he suggests that metaphors must also be "cleared away": "Along the philosophical fringes of science we may find reasons to question basic conceptual structures and to grope for ways to refashion them. Old idioms are bound to fail us here, and only metaphor can begin to limn the new order" (1978: 159).

Goffman's new order is the interaction order, the world of face-to-face interaction. Quine goes on to suggest: "The neatly worked inner stretches of science are an open space in the tropical jungle, created by clearing tropes away" (1978: 160). Quine's argument is that although metaphors are indispensable in the initial phases of scientific work, later they become an unnecessary hindrance. I think that we can identify this development in Goffman's work. Initially, he used the dramaturgical model to "limn the new order"; later he cleared the tropical jungle, replacing it with analytic accounts of the basic elements of face-to-face interaction or what he came to call "the interaction order".

## Unsystematic Observation

It is obvious that sociologists have to observe social interaction and then draw conclusions on the basis of what they
have seen. It is also obvious that if sociologists simply
wrote down everything they saw they would never stop
writing. Just imagine trying to write down everything you
can observe at this moment: you could spend many years
doing this without completing the project. Somewhere in
Robert Pirsig's *Zen and the Art of Motorcycle Maintenance*
one of his characters is asked to describe the town in which
she lives. She tries and fails. Redoubling her efforts, she
tries to describe a building in her town and fails again. In
the end she writes at length about a brick in a building in
her town. Goffman made the same point with deadpan
humor in his dissertation (1953b), carefully describing the
various pool cues in the billiard room in the hotel where he
worked as assistant to the washer-up.

Goffman's naturalistic observations of face-to-face
interaction were unsystematic because they were collected
from different situations as fate allowed. They were also
selective because he chose to focus on certain aspects of
interaction and ignore others. Like Simmel, he watched
people as he and they went about their normal activities
and from this he constructed general descriptions. These
descriptions reorder common observations. They select and
emphasize certain aspects of social interaction, encouraging
us to do the same. Goffman gave us new words, definitions,
and classifications with which to describe face-to-face
interaction. In one sense he discovered things about social
interaction, but in another he invented new ways of looking
at the social world.

Sometimes Goffman emphasized a conceptual schema
and used observations only as confirmatory devices. On
these occasions the data serve to promote the elegance of a
model rather than to describe actual events. When he was
less impressed with his schemata he used observations and

discrepant data to undermine his models, to remind himself and his readers that the social world is much messier than his neat classifications suggest. His work contains many reminders that the complexity of social interaction will not submit to formal analysis. For example, in *Forms of Talk* he ends a chapter about lectures by suggesting that the true role of the lecturer is to give his or her audience respite from the "flickering, cross-purposed, messy irresolution of their unknowable circumstances" (1981a: 195). In *Frame Analysis* he makes fun about his own efforts to specify fundamental rules of everyday behavior, referring to them as the "sociologist's alchemy" (1974: 5).

Nevertheless, all of his books contain elaborate, inter-locking sets of definitions, classifications, and many examples that attempt to describe the social world in formal terms. It is as if he occasionally thought that a neat but oversimplified description of everyday behavior were preferable to a messy but true one.

Goffman's remedy to this dilemma involved a distinctive attitude to discrepant data. Instead of stopping with a set of definitions, classifications, and examples, he assumed that he could improve the analysis by using discrepant observations both to undermine existing definitions and then to suggest new ones. For want of a better name I call this procedure "Goffman's Spiral" (see p. 55) to connote the spiraling back and forth between old and new definitions. The end product is a plurality of attempts to describe face-to-face interaction, each reordering familiar observations in a new way. We can understand the goal of Goffman's Spiral in one of two ways: it could be trying to show that there are many ways of reordering what we know about face-to-face interaction, or it could be trying to find the best way of ordering what we know. The first of these looks like invention, the second discovery.

When describing face-to-face interaction, Goffman reworked his ideas in a way that Baldamus calls "double fitting" (1972). Baldamus has argued that double fitting occurs when empirical examples are chosen or rejected in

order either to confirm existing definitions or to support
the claims of new definitions. He explained double fitting
by an analogy: carpenters would be like sociologists if they
mended a door by altering both the shape of the door and
that of the door frame. Over a period of time it becomes
possible to make some kind of progress and to accumulate
results. In scientific terms, however, he admitted that
double fitting is a way of "cooking the books" (1972: 295).
Later he justified the procedure by saying that combining
the theoretical task of "inventing and articulating conceptual frameworks" with the empirical task of hypothesizing makes it possible to produce an insightful merger of
theory and research (1972: 296–7).

Robin Williams (1988) used Baldamus's idea of double
fitting to make sense of Goffman's methods. Williams
argued that Goffman reordered familiar facts by spiraling
between invention and discovery, between conceptual
elaboration and hypothesizing, between a refocusing of
terms and a refocusing of empirical investigation:

> Sociological discoveries are not then about the anticipated
> or unanticipated discovery of previously unknown facts;
> they are much more about the attribution of different
> significances to what is already known. If sociological
> discoveries are about re-ordering what is already known,
> then sociological methods must be those which permit that
> re-ordering to take place as efficiently and reliably as
> possible. (1988: 73)

Williams believes that Goffman's sociology is a version of
Simmel's and Weber's methodological writings, and he
ended his paper by arguing that Goffman is an heir to
the neo-Kantian conception of the social sciences as the
continuous process of ordering and reordering reality
through the construction, dissolution, and replacement of
concepts (Williams, 1988: 87; Weber, 1949).

In his paper Williams offered a close reading of two
passages from Goffman's corpus, the first from the begin-

ning of Goffman's doctorate, finished in 1953, the second from his final paper, the Presidential Address to the American Sociological Association, these showing very neatly that Goffman did indeed think that during the intervening years he had managed to stabilize "a highly integrated hierarchical structure of interlocking definitions" (1988: 76). Allen Grimshaw offers support for this view, telling us that in his later years Goffman struggled to find ways to systematize his findings (1983: 147). Both Williams and Grimshaw suggest that Goffman wanted to stop the endless process of reordering our descriptions and to settle on one enduring description of face-to-face interaction.

There are clearly many ways of interpreting face-to-face interaction, and to this extent many reorderings are possible. However, within any one of these reorderings there is the prospect of conceptual development and refinement. Goffman developed and refined his ideas by undermining his various definitions or models in order to improve them. He did this by:

1 creating definitions and classifications of face-to-face interaction;
2 focusing on examples that these couldn't accommodate;
3 altering his definitions and classifications to accommodate discrepant examples;
4 focusing on examples that these new definitions couldn't accommodate.

However, throughout Goffman's work there is something troublesome about his use of examples. However "cute" and insightful, his examples always serve the needs of a model. Nothing Goffman says rests on any one example; nor do any of his examples seem to be of particular interest him. To put this issue harshly, his examples are not primarily exemplifications of social behavior; their first goal is to exemplify the usefulness of a *classification* of social behavior. It is this classificatory zeal that gives his books a slightly "flat" feel to them, as Giddens (1987) and others have noticed. Schegloff (1988) pursues this criticism further, arguing that Goffman moves far too rapidly from example to example. Schegloff observes that Goffman rarely finds troublesome data: examples either support a classification or they tell him how to improve it. They are always "just examples" that are instructive but nevertheless disposable.

Ethnomethodologists and conversation analysts have shown that carefully recorded examples can be subjected to very detailed analysis. Their studies show the depth that is sometimes missed by Goffman's swift transitions from example to example. They are also derived from evidence (audio- and audiovisual tapes and transcripts) that can be examined by skeptics. Their findings are therefore subject to peer review.

To sum up this section: Goffman either gave primacy to his various models over his observations or allowed an interplay between model and observation, altering or ignoring elements of both. When he emphasized the model over his observations, he underestimated the importance of detailed, empirical research. When he allowed an interplay between model and observations, he made a pragmatic compromise between analytic neatness and empirical messiness. Baldamus calls this interplay or compromise "double-fitting". I refer to it as "Goffman's Spiral" (see figure on p. 55).

## SYSTEMATIC OBSERVATION: GOFFMAN'S ETHNOGRAPHIC RESEARCH

Goffman's ethnographic methods consist of (1) a standard method of data collection and (2) a distinctive method of data management. The first considers ethnography as a practice, the second as a product, a text. I consider each in turn.

Until very recently it was only possible to speculate about the way Goffman collected data. However, in 1989 the *Journal of Contemporary Ethnography* published a transcript of a talk Goffman gave in 1974 about his field-work methods (Goffman, 1989). Goffman himself did not think that the talk was worthy of publication and so its contents were known only to those with access to bootlegged tapes of the original talk. Permission to publish the transcript was granted by Goffman's widow.

The talk begins with an interesting definition of partici-pant observation as:

> a technique that wouldn't be the only technique a study would employ, it wouldn't be a technique that would be useful for any study, but it's a technique that you can feature in some studies. It's a matter of getting data, it seems to me, by subjecting yourself, your own body and your own personality, and your own social situation, to the set of contingencies that play upon a set of individuals, so that you can physically and ecologically penetrate their circle of response to their social situation, or their ethnic situation, or whatever. (1989: 125)

According to this account, the aim of the participant observer is to understand a culture by tuning one's body to its rhythms, by allowing the routines of a culture to become one's own. Goffman thought that this transformation was the best way of learning both to appreciate the subtleties of a group and to ignore their verbal rationalizations for their actions.

Ethnographers have two problems: "getting into place" and "exploiting place". The first requires a satisfactory justification for informants, one which satisfies their curi-osity. Inadequate justifications will "mess up" a project. Then ethnographers must cut their lives to the bone, separating themselves from outside resources and learning to see the world as informants see it.

As soon as possible, ethnographers should identify the social structure of the group and decide in which of its branches to seek membership. Mobility within the group should only be upwards – otherwise informants will be suspicious. Within these subworlds ethnographers must learn to master little skills which will be initially difficult.

Goffman suggested an informal test of the validity of the research findings:

> there are also little tests that you can run on whether you've really penetrated the society you're studying . . . The sights and sounds around you should get to be normal. You should . . . feel you could settle down and forget about being a sociologist. The members of the opposite sex become attractive to you. You should be able to engage in the same body rhythms, rate of movement, tapping of the feet, that sort of thing, as the people around you. Those are the real tests of penetrating a group. (1989: 129)

The key to exploiting place is to spend at least a year in the field so as to get a full range of events, to triangulate what people say with events and to keep careful notes which honestly describe situations. This honesty is best preserved by not allowing others to read field notes.

Goffman's comments are interesting but not distinctive. The problems of ethnographic data collection have been analyzed in detail by others, and his concerns have been addressed elsewhere. Publication of this talk is noteworthy primarily because it is Goffman's only public record of his views about fieldwork.

The second methodological element is data management. I use this expression to refer to issues to do with the use of field notes. Goffman's overall goal was to transform ethnographies of *places* into ethnographies of *concepts*. He did this by combining engaged and vicarious research in order to produce general findings. His ethnographies offer a new vocabulary with which to practice comparative sociology. This dense summary requires elaboration.

*Asylums* is an unusual ethnography: it contains little background information about the hospital in which the research was conducted, there are no references to or quotations from informants and a significant amount of space is committed to information from a wide variety of sources. The result is an ethnography that is not obviously of a particular place. Instead it is much more accurate to describe *Asylums* as an ethnography of a concept – that of the total institution. Goffman's major interest was to understand the ramifications of an analytic framework; understanding inmate culture at St Elizabeth's hospital was only a secondary consideration. The bulk of *Asylums* develops a set of ideas – a vocabulary – with which to describe the experiences of *any* group of people whose time and space are constantly monitored. Goffman worked out these ideas by finding information on any group whose situation shares a schematic resemblance to that of the institutionalized mentally ill. As a result his ethnography spirals between his own ethnographic findings at St Elizabeth's and the ethnographic findings of other researchers in other settings.

For Goffman, the goals of the ethnographer should be to give a detailed account of a particular group and then to create a framework that will allow comparative research. *Asylums* is an exemplary model of this approach to ethnography.

# 8

# Goffman and Modern Sociology

## INTRODUCTION

Reading Goffman can be frustrating: although his ideas are
fascinating, they also seem to lack an obvious direction. In
this chapter I want to discuss three critical directions for
Goffman's work and their potential impact on modern
sociology. The first concerns the analysis of rules in everyday life, the second concerns the substantive units of face-
to-face interaction, and the third Goffman's contribution to
a general sociological theory.

## RULES RECONSIDERED

Previous chapters introduced the problems which surround
the idea of rule-following in everyday life. In an attempt
to clear these muddy waters, I distinguished rules from
background assumptions and Felicity's Condition. In our
everyday lives, we interpret rules using a set of tacit ideas
about what typically occurs in public settings. These tacit
ideas are background assumptions about the character of

social life. In this book I have called Goffman's analysis of this his SIAC schema. In his later writings, Goffman also analyzed our principal assumption about these assumptions, which, with a jokey reference to John Austin, he called "Felicity's Condition". What is largely missing from Goffman's work, however, is the close study of what we could call "rules in use". Goffman rarely analyzed social situations in detail, preferring instead to write about general issues. The task of analyzing audiovisual material has been undertaken by conversation analysts, some of them Goffman's former students.

As we will see shortly, Goffman overemphasized the extent to which rules constrain or govern behavior. This is a legacy inherited from Durkheim that is of only limited value.

Rules must be distinguished from background assumptions. Rules give specific instruction; background assumptions give guidelines about the range of understandable behavior. Conversation analysis has made significant progress with rules as instructions, Goffman with rules as expectations. These ideas require elaboration.

## RULES AS CONSTRAINTS, RESOURCES, AND INDETERMINATE GUIDES TO ACTION

A lot of sociology is based on the idea that people follow rules which govern or constrain their behavior. Questions about why drivers stop at red lights, why moviegoers queue for tickets or why clumsy people say "*oops!*" seem easiest to answer by saying that in each case people have understood rules which have guided their actions. The task for sociologists then appears to be to decipher the rules that are followed in any interactional episode, however troublesome, illegal, immoral, or inelegant that behavior may seem to outside observers.

This kind of research assumes a structuralist stance for which surface appearances must be understood as the products of underlying rules. This approach is enshrined in Durkheim's *Rules of Sociological Method*, where rules (called "social facts") are thought to be external and independent constraints on the people who follow them. A similar argument pervades Parsons's account of society as a social system maintained by a dominant value consensus. Sociology's sub-specialities often reflect this interest: the "sociology of deviance" studies rule-breaking behavior, "socialization" studies the acquisition of these rules, etc.

For the most part, Goffman assumed that rules are primarily constraints. This assumption is adequate for many empirical projects, since it provides a way of obtaining knowledge about social groups and the norms, values, and rules which govern their activities. However, at other times Goffman emphasized the limitations of the Durkheimian idea that rules are constraints governing behavior, and argued instead that we frequently ignore or abuse rules intended to limit our actions.

On other occasions, Goffman acknowledged the "dance of talk" (1981a: 73), the adaptation and spontaneous manipulation of rules governing behavior. These manipulations are the revenge of the manipulated man on the rules that are meant to manipulate him.

When arguing in this way, Goffman adhered to a model of rules as resources rather than as constraints. Rules not only govern what we say and do, they can also be used by us in what we say and do. They can be honored, inverted, or even disregarded, "depending as the mood strikes" (1981a: 74). The task for sociologists is not simply to codify the rules that people follow in doing what they do, but also to understand how people use these rules for their own purposes.

A brilliant demonstration of this argument is Wieder's study of a halfway house, "Telling the Code" (1974). In the first part of this paper he characterized the "inmate code" in conventional terms, as an informal guide to conduct which is followed by inmates and understood by staff. Rules such as "don't snitch" or "don't cooperate with staff" constrain inmates' behavior and tell them what to do in diverse situations. Thus, when a prison officer asks a new inmate to organize a pool competition, both men know that the offer must be refused.

As this episode reveals, the code offers a way of understanding behavior for both staff and inmates which structures their lives. Wieder put this very well:

> In "telling the code", staff implicitly and explicitly used a wide range of social scientific conceptions, for example rule-governed action, goal-directed action, the distinction between the intended and unintended outcomes of action, the distinction between normatively required and normatively optional means of achieving a morally valued end, roles, role-bound behaviors, and definition of the situation. The use of these ethno-social scientific conceptions in "telling the code" structured staff's environment. It did this by identifying the meaning of a resident's act by placing it in the context of a pattern. (1974: 149)

This passage appears to be saying that the sociological task is to understand the code in the same way that inmates and staff understand it. However, in the second part of the paper, Wieder showed that inmates use the code for their own purposes, and that to this extent they are not constrained by it at all. Inmates and staff can misunderstand situations because of their implicit faith in the code. For some individuals the code can be used as a resource.

Wieder showed this by discussing an incident in which an inmate's bed was burned. For everyone in the halfway house, this episode was interpreted automatically in the context of the code. The fact that a bed caught fire meant that the person who slept there had broken the convict code, and the bed-burning was a symbolic way of initiating punishment against this "deviant". The meaning of this incident was transparent to nearly everyone involved; and however odd to us, the bed-burning could be considered a routine part of institutional life, something easily within the compass of predictable events. The reasoning is simply that the code is broken sometimes and sanctions against offenders are to be expected. This is the nature of rule-governed behavior.

The key to this episode is that the person who set fire to the bed may have known how the incident would be interpreted, and he may have exploited this interpretation in order to mask his own motives. Perhaps he was settling a feud from before their imprisonment, perhaps he just didn't like his victim, perhaps he burned the bed by accident. Whatever the "truth", the convict code did not govern his behavior; he used the code for his own purposes. An analytically similar incident can be observed in bars when men address unknown women by saying "I suppose I shouldn't talk to you without being introduced." Such men use the rule constraining their behavior toward strangers to enable them to do the thing that the rule was intended to prevent.

By combining classical sociology's assumption that rules are skills governing interaction with the realization that rules are also resources used in interaction, a much more interesting account of social life emerges, and one which is important for empirical research, as Wieder demonstrated. However, rules have another important characteristic: they are at best only partial guides to conduct. The partiality of rules is a product of two interrelated factors: their *indexicality* and their *indeterminacy*.

To say that something is indexical means that without supplementary information it is incomprehensible. An indexical expression or rule, therefore, is one which by itself is meaningless, and hence cannot be followed without further instruction. For the most part, we typically think that indexicals are exceptions to the norm, but this is mistaken. In fact, almost everything we say is indexical, from casual questions like "So what do you think about that?" to apparently declarative statements like "My name is Phil Manning." Without additional cultural information these sentences are difficult or impossible to interpret. Any sentence with a reference to a "this" or a "that" obviously requires additional knowledge: consider the skills required in a crowd to fulfill the command to "look at that boy" – and consider how amazing it is that you are often able to find the boy in question. In the second case, sentences naming objects (in the example, me) also require additional knowledge about the frame and context: if I tell you my name in a play it means one thing, at a party, another.

In a famous series of experiments, Garfinkel (1967) showed that we spend our lives tacitly adding information to indexical expressions. Amazingly, for the most part we seem completely unaware of the fact that we do this, and are easily irritated by people who fail to understand, or as Garfinkel puts it, fail to "remedy" our indexical expressions. For example, in one of his experiments Garfinkel asked his students to answer the question, "How are you?" with the reply, "How am I in regard to what? My health, my finances, my personal life?"

We could characterize social life as the continual attempt to remedy a universe of indexicals, as the attempt to supplement signs so as to be able to understand them. When viewed in this way, the ethnomethodologist and the semiotician's understanding of the social world are the same. At the end of *Forms of Talk*, Goffman acknowledges that this "bespeak[s] a trivial game", but reminds us that we spend our lives playing it (1981a: 327). It is instructive in an almost Buddhist-like manner to spend a day watching oneself remedying one indexical expression or rule after another; after a while it is hard to understand how anyone has the time to do anything else.

It is a huge mistake to see the analysis of indexical expressions as trivial, and the research implications are enormous. When sociologists study groups, it is not simply a matter of establishing the rules governing their behavior; instead, the indexicals referring to these rules must somehow be remedied by sociologists in the same way that the subjects themselves remedy them. This is likely to be very difficult, principally, but not only, because the subjects themselves may not know discursively how they make sense of various indexicals – they just "know" what something means in a practical way. Worse, sociologists typically find that their questions are seen as intrusive or strange, as Goffman noted in his dissertation: "In order to learn what the right questions were, I had to become taken for granted by the community to a degree and in a way that made it unsuitable for me to ask these questions" (1953b: 5).

Indexicality has a creeping quality. At first it seems to be false because there are some "obvious" sentences or rules whose meanings are transparent. The mistaken assumption that self-sufficient sentences or rules exist shows us how adept we are at interpreting indexicals (so adept, indeed, that we overlook the fact that we *did* interpret them through the addition of significant amounts of information). These sorts of thought experiments show that indexicals exist and that we constantly decipher them. However, they still tend to appear as trivial features of the social world, unworthy of attention. Their enormous significance is only apparent when sociologists experience difficulty in deciphering the interactions of members of various subcultures. At such times, the complexity of remedying indexicals seems awe-inspiring. Indeed, perhaps the only thing which is more awe-inspiring is that for those within these subcultures the remedying of indexicals is achieved so easily. For them, it is an invisible accomplishment. Perhaps we could compare this skill to that of jazz musicians who improvise musical scores: to us this seems overwhelmingly difficult, to them it seems child's play.

Ethnomethodologists have explored the issue of indexicality in great detail, as they have the second issue linked to rule-following – their indeterminacy. We typically think of rules as instructions such as: "in circumstances x, y, and z, do a"; or "in all circumstances, do a." Etiquette books are examples of this way of thinking. In *Behavior in Public Places* (1963a), for example, Goffman discussed the advice that when introduced to an armless man, one should shake his stump. In this and other less delicate situations, there is an unproblematic assumption that rules match acts to circumstances. However, there are a significant number of occasions in which this mechanical account of social interaction breaks down, and the rules that participants attempt to follow only give partial instruction.

Once again, Wieder is an excellent guide to this problem. Part of the inmate code was to avoid cooperation with staff, and therefore an inmate asked by an officer to organize a pool competition is clearly in a circumstance in which his response is governed by the code. However, when Wieder approached the inmates with questions, the code offered them indeterminate guidance since Wieder's status was vague: clearly he is not a staff member (he is not even obviously an authority figure); and yet he is also clearly not an inmate. Wieder found that even inmates who wanted to use the code were prevented from so doing by this uncertainty. They discovered that there was not an obvious way of conforming to (or deviating from) the code, and they were left alone to decide both whether to talk to Wieder and whether that talk would be in violation of the code (Wieder, 1974: 155).

This view is either implicitly or explicitly indebted to Wittgenstein's *Philosophical Investigations* (1972), where he uses a series of thought experiments to challenge common assumptions about rules and rule-following. These experiments suggest, albeit elliptically, that we shouldn't guess about rules of everyday behavior but should look and see how they are used. Similarly, we shouldn't expect a mathematical clarity in our formulations of rules. Rules are used in murky everyday settings where they are subject to many contingencies. It is common for there to be doubt about how to follow a rule.

Rawls (1989) has suggested that philosophical debates about rules are an important guide to the differences between Goffman and conversation analysts. Rawls argues that Goffman usually assumes that rules are constraints that are sustained through interaction, and that are therefore internal to social interaction (1989: 154). Rawls calls this the "constitutive production" of order. Goffman provides the vocabulary necessary to analyze this, although he rarely produced detailed analyses of particular episodes of interaction (Schegloff, 1988). Rawls continues by arguing that

> The problem with Goffman's position is that no matter how large the number of categories one has for interpreting intended speaker–hearer relations which would in turn shed light on the meaning of utterances, there is still a degree of ambiguity which the categories cannot disambiguate. This is the perennial problem with explaining language via rules and categories. No matter how finely we try to pin down the meaning of words and rules, there is always room left for interpretation. (1989: 158)

In this passage Rawls points out that even when we try to follow rules we do so in ways that are ambiguous. This ambiguity exists in part because the rules we are trying to follow are indeterminate. The task of giving a full account of a rule leads to infinite regress. In everyday life, people experience this as a problem of wanting to know that they have been understood. The best guide they have to this is the sequential relevance demonstrated by next speaker's turn at talk; that is, by second speaker showing an understanding of first speaker's talk. This demonstration is a practical rather than a theoretical demonstration: we assume that second speaker's comments really are sequentially relevant, and only very strange comments challenge this assumption. This practical approach to language is a routine way of side-stepping an insoluble dilemma.

## RULES AND SOCIAL INTERACTION: A SUMMARY

Developing an understanding of rule following behavior is a major task for sociology. Major schools of thought, including functionalism and ethnomethodology, can be distinguished on the basis of their assumptions about the nature of rules in everyday life. In this and previous chapters I have made a series of claims in an attempt to synthesize different findings relating to rules and social interaction:

1  Rules should be distinguished from both background assumptions and from Felicity's Condition (Goffman's term for our assumption about our assumptions).

2  Background assumptions tell us what to expect in the wide range of encounters that constitute the interaction order, but they do not tell us what to do.

3  There are four principal background assumptions: Situational Propriety, Involvement, Accessibility, and Civil Inattention (SIAC).

4  SIAC assumes the routine maintenance of Felicity's Condition, which requires us to demonstrate the sanity underlying our social interaction.

5  Background assumptions tell us what to expect, rules tell us what to *do*.

6  There are different forms of rules: formal, ceremonial, constitutive, regulative, symmetrical, and asymmetrical.

7  Following Wittgenstein, rule-following should be understood as a skill.

8  Rules are sometimes constraints that govern our conduct.

9  Rules are sometimes resources used by people for their own purposes.

10  Rules are indeterminate guides to action that are inherently indexical.

## THE SUBSTANTIVE UNITS OF FACE-TO-FACE INTERACTION

The identification of the basic units of face-to-face interaction is a continual theme of Goffman's work. In his
Presidential Address (1983b) he described this project as
the study of the "interaction order": "My concern over the
years has been to promote acceptance of this face-to-face
domain as an analytically viable one – a domain which
might be titled, for want of any happy name, the *interaction
order* – a domain whose preferred method of study is
microanalysis" (1983b: 2). There is something very satis-
fying about his decision to describe face-to-face interaction
as the interaction order, since he first used this term as the
title to the conclusion of his dissertation (1953b). It is a
symbol of the consistency of his agenda. It also emphasizes
his belief that heterogeneous occasions of face-to-face
conduct have generic properties.

It is instructive either to listen to a recording of an
apparently simple conversation or to scrutinize a videotape
of an apparently routine strip of social interaction: you
discover that there are intricate patterns and important
nuances in everything we say and do. The mundane world
cannot look the same again. In order to analyze the patterns and nuances of social interaction it is necessary to
categorize the different types of things that occur when
people come into each other's presence. Some basic
classificatory work is required.

Watching a videotape of mundane interaction is the
easiest way of understanding the importance of discovering
substantive units. Without the help of such units, it is very
difficult to describe what is happening on the screen.
Goffman assumed that social interaction is constructed out
of a series of routine procedures and assumptions that we
should be able to categorize. The ensuing analysis will
be very complicated and require considerable detail.
Nevertheless, by combining elements from his different

books it is clear that Goffman thought that there were basic elements of the interaction order. These will be the tools needed to describe and then interpret face-to-face inter-action. These units are:

1    spatial units;
2    verbal and non-verbal communication;
3    participation units;
4    system and ritual constraints.

Goffman's work addressed these issues continually, albeit unsystematically. In the future it may be possible to unite them into a general description of the elements of face-to-face interaction. This project will require extensive inter-disciplinary collaboration.

### 1    Spatial Units

The basic spatial unit of the interaction order is the *social situation* – any arena of mutual monitoring. There are two types of social situation: *occasions* and *gatherings*: the first is part of a wider event, such as a cocktail party, the second stands by itself. The interaction in social situations is *focused* if there is a single claim on attention or *unfocused* if the interaction is simply based on co-presence. Thus, interaction in a meeting is focused, in an elevator un-focused (1963a: 18–23). Interaction is noticeably different in these different settings. Thus, for example, in focused occasions such as meetings we act in one way and in un-focused gatherings such as corridors we act in another. He also specified a range of uses of space within social situations.

In *Relations in Public* (1971) Goffman distinguished various "territories of the self", some of which are types of space within social situations. The first is the "personal space" that surrounds individuals, marking an encroachment zone. Typically, we are more sensitive to intrusions into the space in front of us, and insensitive to happenings behind our backs. The desired amount of personal space varies from setting to setting: in a commuter train it is small, in an empty lecture theater large (1971: 52–4). The second unit of space is the "stall", which is any fixed and demarcated area to which individuals can attach a temporary claim, such as telephone booths or restaurant tables. The third unit is "use space": the space in front of someone, which is needed to complete a task, such as the space between a picture and a visitor to the gallery in which it hangs. The fourth unit is the "sheath", the space physically occupied by someone. Fifth is "possessional territory" – the space occupied by objects clearly belonging to someone nearby, and which thereby mark out territory (1971: 52–65). This analysis is underdeveloped and not coordinated with the earlier delineation of social situations, even though it is an attempt to specify the use of space within them. Significant amounts of analytic and empirical research are needed. In the first place, the findings of a range of social scientists need to be integrated. Disciplinary barriers have slowed down this integration.

## 2   *Verbal and Non-verbal Communication*

For Goffman, both verbal and non-verbal face-to-face interaction is made up of *moves*. In his "Face-work" essay he defined a move as "everything conveyed by an actor during a turn at taking action" (1955: 20). Moves consist of (1) messages, (2) ritual respect, (3) face-work, (4) communicative constraints, and (5) framing instructions. All this takes place within the limitations set by "Felicity's Condition": that is, by our need to demonstrate meaning and sanity in what we say and do (see chapter 4).

Messages are the information that the "sender" wants to send to the "receiver". Ritual respect and face-work are interrelated: the former shows regard for others, the latter for self. Pride is sustained and shame avoided through ritual exchanges. Communicative constraints consist of the requirements that speakers must meet if their "moves" are to be understood. Framing instructions are the "messages about the message" that give recipients an interpretation schema, such as joke or sad story. Goffman's work suggests that, ironically, the message, the apparent reason for the communication, is a relatively small part of the interactional move.

Our actions consist of a series of verbal and non-verbal moves that convey many things. For example, when the captain of a 747 says that the plane will land 15 minutes behind schedule, she will probably do so in a way that conveys a message, that reminds us of her professional and not gendered status (perhaps by a self-reference to a title such as "captain"), that pays deference to us as valued passengers, that is easily understood (i.e. as a comment about not just any plane but the plane that is flying at the moment), and that is framed to be a serious comment. If we were able to see the pilot do this as well as hear her do it, we might also observe non-verbal signs indicating that the flight's lateness does not stop this from being just another routine activity that she has performed many times before. In addition, we might also see that her role as captain, in which we invest trust, money, and our lives, is one that she finds somewhat limiting, and this too might be signaled in her body language.

There are still fundamental problems with Goffman's concept of a primary framework that need to be resolved. Goffman's analysis of interactional moves requires considerable amounts of detailed research, and his work as it stands is only suggestive. A similar comment can be made about his analysis of embarrassment, pride, and shame.

### 3   *Participation Units*

Goffman argued that social interaction happens in spaces that usually affect how we act in them and that this might be amenable to classification. His classification distinguished social situations, occasions, and gatherings, and also focused and unfocused situations. The analysis to this point is already complicated, and it has not yet considered the different categories of participant in the interaction order. He attempted to specify these substantive units at various points through *Relations in Public* (1971), *Frame Analysis* (1974), and *Forms of Talk* (1981a).

In *Relations in Public*, Goffman suggested that participants in social situations are either "single" or in a "with". A single is a person standing alone, a with is a party of two or more who are perceived to be "together" (1971: 41). It is generally easier for strangers to approach singles than withs, which raises the question of participant ratification. Participants are not equally free to speak to anyone at anytime; instead, their participation has to be ratified by those present. This allows us to consider the "production format", "participation status", and "participation framework" of social interaction (1981: 137).

Beginning with the simple distinction between speaker and hearer, Goffman devised a "production format" for speakers. His first description of the production format is buried in a footnote in *Relations in Public*, where he commented that people sometimes "clown . . . a character" not their own, allowing themselves to be ventriloquized, their assumption being, perhaps, that "real rules only apply to real people" (1971: 155, footnote). And later in the same chapter he outlined the argument that became the "Footing" paper in *Forms of Talk* (1981a):

> . . . the individual does not go about merely going about his business. He goes about constrained to sustain a viable image of himself in the eyes of others. . . . Each lurching of

whatever the individual is standing on will have to be offset, often by his leading into the fall with a self that has been projected as unserious, the real person thereby made free to tacitly take up a counterbalancing position. (1971: 223)

These observations prepare the ground for the more sophisticated accounts offered in *Frame Analysis* and *Forms of Talk*, which analyzed the ways in which we often appear to be both "ventriloquist" and "puppet" at the same time. In order to explain the way in which we separate ourselves from what we're saying, Goffman classified different types of speaker. This classification is the production format of face-to-face interaction.

In *Frame Analysis* he distinguished four categories:

1   the *principal* – the person or party held responsible for the position attested to by the meaning of what was spoken;
2   the *emitter* – the "actual sounding box" – the speaking entity;
3   the *animator* – the expressive actions accompanying talk;
4   the *figure* – the human or non-human characters enacted by the speaker. (1974: 517–23)

A person frequently enacts all of these different speakers at the same time. In "Footing" he reworked this analysis, running together the notions of "emitter" and "animator", and distinguishing "principal" from "author"; the former being the position established by the speaker, the latter the creator of that position. Taken together Goffman called the animator, author, and principal the "production format" (1981b: 144–5). The notion of the "figure" was kept, although left out of this definition (1981b: 147). The result of the conceptual elaboration is the loosening of the connection between the identity of speakers and their talk. Goffman made the point graphically: ". . . although it will never be that a two-headed green man from Mars will debate with the ghost of Andrew Jackson, it is structurally just as easy during real talk to replay a purported scene between these two as it is to replay a conversation which occurred that morning with the postman" (1974: 524).

Conversation analysts have realized that participation units are critical to many of their own research projects. An excellent example of this Maynard's (1984) study of plea-bargaining. Maynard analyzes the day-to-day work of attorneys trying to .reach pretrial agreements about sentences. He shows that pleabargaining is achieved by a series of interactional shifts by attorneys; i.e. they change their production formats. Thus, when a district attorney (DA) says to the public defendant (PD) "I've got an offer that I'll make at this time" the PD has to decide whether the DA is the principal or the animator of the sentence. As a principal, the DA is simply expressing a personal opinion, whereas the DA as animator is representing the legal view of the office of the district attorney (Maynard, 1984: 57).

### 4   System and Ritual Constraints

Interactional moves contain a lot of information that can be misinterpreted or misheard, with the result that reruns or rephrasings are needed. There is, Goffman suggested, a "basic normative assumption" that participants in social interaction should be able to agree as to what they heard and saw (1981a: 10). If they can't agree, then "repairs" will be necessary, sometimes by the speaker, sometimes by the hearer or hearers. In order to minimize the necessity of repair, there are constraints on how interactants make their moves, particularly regarding their talk. Goffman called these "system constraints", identifying eight of them:

1  two-way acoustically adequate system;
2  back-channel feedback capabilities;
3  contact signals announcing beginning and end of communication;

4   turnover signals;
5   preemption or repair signals;
6   framing capabilities;
7   norms inducing honesty;
8   nonparticipant constraints. (1981: 14–15)

This model is a significant advance over the one pro-
posed in his dissertation, which simply looked at the
sender's need to know that the message had been received
by the intended recipient (1953b). This new model, which
is a version of the turn-taking system outlined by Sacks,
Schegloff, and Jefferson (1974), allows a much more detailed analysis. This is an important area in which Goffman
is indebted to the work of some of his former students,
particularly Sacks and Schegloff.

On first inspection, many of the elements of Goffman's
model of system constraints look trivial, and it is only
later that their importance can be understood. The first
constraint, that messages can be heard, is clearly a prerequisite for communication. The second, howevei, that
back-channel must be possible is less obvious but no less
important. Speakers listen carefully to the little sounds
that hearers make, interpreting them to mean that their
words have been understood and that they should continue
speaking. Should back-channel be halted for any reason,
speakers worry that they are speaking only to themselves.
This feedback can be verbal, done through expressions
such as "uh-huh" or it can be non-verbal, done through a
nodding of the head. In phone calls, verbal back-channel
feedback has to be extensive owing to the impossibility
of any other kind of sign that hearer wants speaker to
continue speaking. There must also be contact signals
to affirm that talk can begin and end. Without them,
possible recipients of talk are forced to ask interactionally
embarrassing questions such as, "Are you talking to me?"
Similarly, there must be ways of both signaling that it
is time for someone else to speak and that the previous
message has not been received. In addition, there must be
cues that tell interactants about the operative frame and

any keyings thereof, and when required, interactants must have ways of making each other speak honestly, and ways of ensuring that they do so for the benefit of only ratified participants.

In addition to system constraints there are ritual constraints that require us to display at least a perfunctory regard for other people and the roles they perform. Ritual constraints sanction us to reproduce this ritual order. Goffman identified three such constraints:

1 To project information about oneself and one's relationships to others present.

2 To remedy offensive or potentially offensive acts to the satisfaction of the offended parties.

3 To induce remedies from those unwilling to supply them (1981a: 21).

The notion of ritual constraints reminds us of a lesson from *Interaction Ritual*: that although communication appears to be at issue, it would be more accurate to say that the main concern is our conduct (1967: 134). When this is questionable, remedial work follows, in the form of accounts, apologies, or requests.

Remedial work is designed to mitigate a worst-possible reading of our conduct. Accounts do so by pleading unusual circumstances in an effort to "explain away" inappropriate behavior. By contrast, apologies acknowledge the wayward conduct, but then separate the apologizer into a guilty and an outraged party, with the latter apologizing for the former. Apologies are often perceived to be compensatory, but in fact they are attempts to affirm relationships. As a result, apologies aren't open to gradation: whether you run over someone's sentence, time, or dog, you have little choice but to say a variation of "I'm sorry" (1971: 149). Both accounts and apologies should be distinguished from requests, which are made before the offense for which remedial work will be necessary. In order to be tactful, we often make pre-requests, such as the paradoxical "Can I ask you a question?" (1971: 146). In this example, tact demands both an unaskable and an unanswerable question.

This analytic schema of the units of the interaction order is only meant to suggest that it should be possible to find a common framework for a wide range of studies of face-to-face interaction. It is clearly beyond the scope of this project to discuss the details of such a framework. However, its development will strengthen our basic understanding of everyday life.

## GOFFMAN AND SOCIAL THEORY

The account of rules that emerged in the first part of this chapter emphasized that a Durkheimian view of rules as external constraints is misleading; and that sophisticated analyses of social life have shown that rule-following is an activity that is achieved in interaction by participants who are knowledgeable about both the rules they should follow and their own ability to manipulate these rules. Rules are enmeshed in assumptions about interaction. This entanglement combines the two questions: "What should I expect?" and "What should I do?" The first question is answered by Goffman's SIAC schema, the second by the detailed analyses developed by ethnomethodologists and conversation analysts. Expected behavior that is in accordance with rules can be parodied by making the rules to be followed a topic for the interaction that is meant to be constrained by them. This reminds us of the pervasive reflexivity of social life.

As this analysis stands, social encounters are regarded as a series of analytically discrete events for which research only needs a videotape or brief transcript. This is because the rules to be studied are displayed each time in each segment of social interaction. The ensuing analysis can and must be indifferent to questions of history, social structure, and individual character, since these concerns are not tied explicitly to rule-following. This type of research has many practical advantages: it is simple to tape and transcribe a conversation.

In *Interaction Ritual* Goffman suggested a more formal justification for this kind of work: "I assume that the proper study of interaction is not the individual and his psychology, but rather the syntactical relations among the acts of different persons mutually present to one another. . . . Not, then, men and their moments. Rather moments and their men" (1967: 2–3).

However, although for some sociological purposes the study of rules can proceed unhindered by wider social concerns, for others this is a severe handicap, and this has become the focus of criticism for many of Goffman's detractors. A similar criticism can, of course, be raised against ethnomethodological and conversation analytic work. There are situations in which a concentration on rules is unable to answer research questions, and in these situations a conceptual bridge is needed to wider concerns. Goffman's solution to this problem was to develop two related ideas, those of *role* and *career*. For these terms he was indebted to the symbolic-interactionist ideas prevalent at Chicago during his graduate research.

Goffman warned us that the meaning of the term "role" wavers when scrutinized carefully, but that it can be initially defined as "the activity the incumbent would engage in were he to act solely in terms of the normative demands upon someone in that position" (1961b: 75). Goffman defined the term "career" as "any social strand of any person's course through life", continuing to say that the focus should concern aspects that are "basic and common" to those sharing the same career (1961a: 119).

The introduction of these two terms allowed Goffman to make three advances:

1 The terms "roles" and "careers" link face-to-face social interaction to the production and reproduction of social structures.

2 By analyzing roles and careers as elements of a social

structure, it becomes possible to analyze relations of power (this idea links roles to asymmetrical rules).

3   Roles give us a sense of the identities of rule-followers (the men and women as well as their moments).

Goffman's role analysis is an attempt to understand the relationship between individuals and the behavior which is expected of them. As with rules, these role-expectations can be understood as both external constraints on the occupant of the role *and* as resources to be manipulated by the role-player.

In *The Presentation of Self*, roles are thought of as fabricated performances, staged either for the benefit or at the expense of various audiences. Performances can be either cynical or sincere, depending on whether the performer believes in the part being played. They are always accompanied by a "front", which defines the situation. A front is usually a combination of "setting" (perhaps a professional office), "expressive equipment" (clothes, speech, etc.), and "manner", the stimuli which warn audience about the nature of upcoming performances.

Goffman considered the idea of a role more extensively in his "Role Distance" paper (1961b), which hinges on the distinctions between role *commitment*, role *attachment*, role *embracement*, and role *distance*. Role commitment refers to roles which are imposed on the individual, role attachment to those we wish to play, role embracement to those roles whose "virtual self" we freely adopt, and role distance to roles from whose virtual self we wish to remain separate. Goffman used the idea of a virtual self to refer to our expectations about the character possessed by a person in a certain role.

These four terms are very useful descriptive tools. For example, consider the claim that people who inject heroin are playing the role of drug addict. Using these terms it is possible to distinguish, for example, addicts who are committed to the role because their body craves the drug from addicts who are attached to the role because they perceive it to symbolize an exciting life of "ripping and running" (Agar, 1973). It is important to note that a person could be attached to the role of heroin addict without ever taking the drug, since role attachment denotes the desire rather than the ability to play the role. Addicts embrace the role of drug addict when they are committed, attached, and actively involved in playing the role (to be actively involved means to accept the self which is thought to accompany the role). There is a test given to drug addicts, the first question of which is "Who are you?". Heroin addicts reply by saying "I am a heroin addict" – i.e. they embrace the role, they acknowledge this identity. Goffman explained this type of comment by saying that "to embrace a role is to be embraced by it", giving examples of baseball managers during games and traffic policemen at busy intersections (1961b: 94).

The term "role distance" describes individuals who are attached and committed to a role, but who wish to distance themselves from the identity that accompanies it. For such people, roles seem to be challenges to their sense of identity and individuality. Role distance is a way of preserving a sense that there is an "I" who is different from all the other occupants and players of a role. It produces a "wedge" between the person and the role which allows him to accept the role on his own terms, and to deny the virtual self that is typically thought to be part of the role (1961b: 95). Combining analyses of social structure with studies of face-to-face interaction has been an enduring problem for sociology. Role analysis seems the principal way of achieving this synthesis.

Finding this kind of a synthesis is a perennial problem for sociologists. In the absence of this synthesis, sociologists work with a confusing array of different paradigms. It may be accurate to say that sociology in the 1990s resembles biology in the 1940s before the discovery of DNA. Since the 1950s biology has been able to develop at a rapid pace, thanks primarily to the collaborative research made possible by general confidence in their paradigm. Perhaps sociology is on the verge of a paradigmatic breakthrough. Unfortunately, it is impossible to know that sociologists are only a few years behind biologists, and it could be that we are now where they were not in 1940 but in 1840. Optimism is needed.

A general theory or paradigm for sociology must account for more than face-to-face interaction, and therefore Goffman's work can only be one among several elements contributing to this project. The only sustained attempt to construct such a theory using Goffman's work is Giddens's structuration theory (1984). Over twenty years Giddens has attempted to integrate different schools of sociological thought. The details of his project are beyond the scope of this book; nevertheless, it is important to consider the skeleton of Giddens's account because they suggest that Goffman's work may be much more important than Goffman himself realized.

Giddens believes that sociologists face a common set of concerns irrespective of their particular substantive interests or methodological preferences. He has therefore attempted to create a framework for sociological investigation that focuses on precisely these concerns. This framework helps sociologists to organize their ideas and findings. Goffman plays a significant role in this theory, although he does so in ways which were not of particular interest to him. The complexities of the interaction order – of face-to-face interaction – occupied Goffman fully, and he did not concern himself with the problems facing sociology in general.

Giddens claims that sociologists have usually offered one of two descriptions of human behavior without realizing that each is inextricable from the other. The first interprets human behavior as an occasion of face-to-face interaction, the second as an example of the functioning of a social system, where the social system is thought of as a pattern of relationships, as found in a nation-state, an organization, or a social group. In the first case there is an emphasis on individuals sustaining and creating meaningful relationships, in the second an emphasis on the interaction between different elements of a social system, typically through the enactment of certain roles. Both possess obvious drawbacks and limitations.

For a sociological analysis to be satisfactory, Giddens argues that it must demonstrate a connection between face-to-face interaction and the organized pattern of role relationships that constitute a social system. In Giddens's vocabulary, sociologists must demonstrate a connection between "social integration" and "system integration". Social integration refers to the interactions between knowledgeable individuals that produce an organized and predictable series of face-to-face exchanges. System integration refers to the interactions between the different parts of a social system that produce a continual sense of social order over time. This distinction is not as abstract and forbidding as it appears at first. Consider a sociological analysis of a large corporation: system integration is maintained through the relationships between different roles in the corporation; social integration is maintained through face-to-face interaction.

Both face-to-face relationships and the relationships between the different parts of a social system are "structured", by which Giddens means that they are produced and reproduced through the application of "rules and resources".* Rules are the formal and informal skills needed to carry on a lifestyle or career, whether professional or deviant in character. At the level of face-to-face interaction, these rules are the skills that Goffman and the ethnomethodologists have brought to our attention.

---

* Readers should be aware of a possible confusion. I use the word "resources" to describe the activity of using assumptions about rules for personal goals. Giddens uses the term in a completely different context. My account of rule-following does bear a resemblance to his discussion of the "reflexive monitoring" of social action and sociology's "double hermeneutic" (Giddens, 1984). Here I have tried to present a bare skeleton of the key elements of structuration theory, and so have deliberately avoided these fleshy details.

Rules at the level of system integration concern the relationships between the different roles performed by an organization, a group, or even a nation-state. Resources are inseparable from rules: they are the ability to control either people or things. Giddens calls the first of these "authoritative resources", the second "allocative resources". In both cases, the structuring of social and system integration both enables and constrains social action, and is therefore always a display of power. That the social world is a hugely predictable environment is a tremendous collective achievement and not the byproduct of an externally constraining social system.

Although Giddens draws heavily on Goffman for his analysis of social integration, he is also indebted to ethnomethodology, conversation analysis, and symbolic interactionism. Giddens focuses on the widespread agreements between these approaches and plays down their differences. I think his assumption of compatibility is a positive and pragmatic leap towards the much needed integration of these schools of thought.

Although there are a variety of attempts to combine analyses of face-to-face interaction and institutional action, there has not been a credible way of achieving this goal. Giddens's solution is to offer a radical interpretation of time and space as the key to this dilemma. This interpretation demonstrates a relationship between Goffman's analysis of social interaction among people who are co-present and institutional analyses in which social interaction occurs among people who are separated in time and space. Giddens notes that many, perhaps most, social relationships occur in situations in which the participants are absent. For example, I rent an apartment but have never met my landlord; I work in a university but have never met the man whose signature approves my contract each year; I have a bank account but have only met the bank teller who accepted my application. In more extensive ways than are at first imaginable, we are all implicated in significant relationships with people whom we have never met.

Giddens calls this phenomenon "disembedding", a term which characterizes very well the way modern life is experienced through vicarious relationships (1990: 21–9).

We must and do possess a large amount of trust in these relationships. This trust is a show of confidence in "symbolic tokens" such as money and in the "expert systems" of professional competence that are essential to the maintenance of an industrial society (1990: 22). Giddens has recently explored these issues in some detail. To realize their importance, consider a family home: although it may appear to be a familiar environment, it could only be constructed by the combined efforts of many expert systems, involving architectural, electrical, and numerous other knowledge bases. For each of these there is a considerable potential for danger, and yet we all live in these environments without significant stress. Indeed, to seek confirmation of the safety of an expert system, perhaps by asking to see a bus driver's license or a physician's medical-school grades, would be a display of situational impropriety. The notion of an expert system is closely tied to the abstract characteristics of a role. Social life is therefore experienced through the interweaving of social relationships of presence and absence.

Giddens's radicalized conception of space, time, and structure is a dazzling attempt to overcome traditional sociological distinctions between macro- and micro-sociological theorizing. It uses Goffman in ways that Goffman himself had not foreseen. The critical question now concerns the success of empirical projects adopting a structurationist stance. It is necessary to show, as Giddens puts it, that the theory is effective as a "sensitizing device" for empirical researchers (1989: 294).

Without usurping the importance of empirical research and without expressing methodological preferences, Giddens has used Goffman as part of a summary of the critical issues facing sociological analysis. Irrespective of the success of this project, Goffman will remain very important for sociology. However, should Giddens succeed in establishing a general theory, Goffman will emerge as a founder of an eagerly awaited general paradigm for modern sociology.

# Bibliography*

## COMPREHENSIVE BIBLIOGRAPHIES OF WORK BY OR RELATING TO GOFFMAN

DITTON, J. (ed.) 1980. *The View From Goffman*, London and Basingstoke: Macmillan.

DREW, P., and WOOTTON, A. (eds) 1988. *Erving Goffman: Exploring the Interaction Order*, Cambridge: Polity.

"Erving Goffman's Sociology" (special issue) *Human Studies* 1989, Vol. 12, Nos. 1–2.

## ERVING GOFFMAN'S WRITINGS

GOFFMAN, E. 1949. "Some Characteristics of Response to Depicted Experience". MA Thesis, University of Chicago.

—— 1951. "Symbols of Class Status", *British Journal of Sociology*, Vol. 11, pp. 294–304.

—— 1952. "On Cooling the Mark Out: Some Aspects of Adaptation to Failure", *Psychiatry*, Vol. 15, No. 4 (November), pp. 451–63.

—— 1953a. "The Service Station Dealer: The Man and His Work", Chicago: Social Research Inc.

—— 1953b. "Communication Conduct in an Island Community" (unpublished Ph.D. thesis, University of Chicago.

*The bibliography contains only material considered in this book.

—— 1955. "On Face-work: An analysis of ritual elements in social interaction". *Psychiatry: Journal for the Study of Interpersonal Processes*, Vol. 18, No. 3 (August), pp. 213–231.

—— 1956a. *The Presentation of Self in Everyday Life*, University of Edinburgh Social Sciences Research Centre, Monograph No. 2.

—— 1956b. "The Nature of Deference and Demeanor", *American Anthropologist*, Vol. 58, No. 3 (June), pp. 473–502.

—— 1956c. "Embarrassment and Social Organization", *American Journal of Sociology*, Vol. 62(3) (November), pp. 264–71.

—— 1957. "Alienation from Interaction", *Human Relations*, Vol. 10, No. 1 (January), pp. 47–59.

—— 1959. *The Presentation of Self in Everyday Life*, Harmondsworth: Penguin.

—— 1961a. *Asylums*, Harmondsworth: Penguin.

—— 1961b. *Encounters: Two Studies in the Sociology of Interaction*, Indianapolis: Bobbs-Merill.

—— 1963. *Behavior in Public Places: Notes on the Social Organization of Gatherings*, New York: The Free Press.

—— 1964a. *Stigma*, Englewood Cliffs, NJ: Prentice-Hall.

—— 1964b. "The Neglected Situation", *American Anthropologist*, Vol. 66, pp. 133–6.

—— 1967. *Interaction Ritual: Essays on Face-to-Face Behavior*, New York: Anchor.

—— 1970. *Strategic Interaction*, Oxford: Basil Blackwell.

—— 1971. *Relations in Public: Microstudies of the Public Order*, New York: Basic Books.

—— 1974. *Frame Analysis: An Essay on the Organization of Experience*, New York: Harper and Row.

—— 1977. "The Arrangement Between the Sexes", *Theory and Society*, Vol. 4, No. 3, pp. 301–32.

—— 1979. *Gender Advertisements*, London: Macmillan.

—— 1981a. *Forms of Talk*, Oxford: Basil Blackwell.

—— 1981b. "Reply to Denzin and Keller", *Contemporary Sociology*, Vol. 10, pp. 60–8.

—— 1983a. "Felicity's Condition", *American Journal of Sociology*, Vol. 89, No. 1, pp. 1–53.

—— 1983b. "The Interaction Order", *American Sociological Review*, Vol. 48, pp. 1–17.

—— 1989. "On Fieldwork", *Journal of Contemporary Ethnography*, Vol. 18, No. 2, pp. 123–32.

## GENERAL REFERENCES

AGAR, M. 1973. *Ripping and Running. A Formal Ethnography of Heroin Addicts*, New York: Seminar Press.

ANDERSON, R., and SHARROCK, W. 1982. "Sociological Work: Some Proceduers Sociologists Use for Organizing Phenomena", *Social Analysis*, No. 11 (October).

ATKINSON, J., and HERITAGE, J. 1984. *Structures of Social Action*, Cambridge: Cambridge University Press.

AUSTIN, J. 1976. *How to Do Things with Words*, Oxford: Oxford University Press.

BALDAMUS, W. 1972. "The Role of Discoveries in Social Science" in T. Shanin (ed.), *The Rules of the Game*, London: Tavistock.

—— 1977. *The Structure of Sociological Inference*, London and Basingstoke: Macmillan.

BATAILLE, G. 1982. *Story of the Eye*, Harmondsworth: Penguin.

BERMAN, M. 1972. "Weird But Brilliant Light on the Way We Live Now", *New York Times Review of Books* (27 February).

BLACK, M. 1962. *Models and Metaphors*, Cornell: Cornell University Press.

BLUMER, H. 1937. "Symbolic Interactionism" in E. P. Schmidt (ed.), *Man and Society*, New York: Prentice-Hall.

—— 1969. *Symbolic Interactionism: Perspective and Method*, Englewood Cliffs, NJ: Prentice-Hall.

—— 1972. "Action" vs. "Interaction", *Society*, Vol. 9 (April), pp. 50–3.

BOOTH, W. 1979. "Metaphor as Rhetoric: The Problem of Evaluation" in S. Sacks (ed.), *On Metaphor*. Chicago: Chicago University Press.

BRAND, S. 1987. *The Media Lab*. New York: Penguin Books.

BROWN, R. 1977. *A Poetic for Sociology*. Cambridge: Cambridge University Press.

BURKE, K. 1955. *Permanence and Change*. Indianapolis: Bobbs-Merrill.

CIOFFI, F. 1969–70. "Information, Contemplation and Social Life", *Royal Institute of Philosophy Lectures*, Vol. 4, pp. 103–31.

COHEN, T. 1979. "Metaphor and the Cultivation of Intimacy" in S. Sacks (ed.), *On Metaphor*.

COLLINS, R. 1980. "Erving Goffman and the Development of Modern Social Theory" in J. Ditton (ed.), 1980.

—— 1988. "Theoretical Continuities in Goffman's Work" in P. Drew and A. Wootton (eds).

CONRAD, P., and SCHNEIDER, J. 1980. *Deviance and Medicalization: From Badness to Sickness*. St Louis: C. V. Mosby.

COOPER, D. 1985. "Metaphors We Live By" in A. Phillips Griffiths, *Philosophy and Practice*, Cambridge: Cambridge University Press.

DAVIDSON, D. 1979. "What Metaphors Mean" in S. Sacks (ed.), *On Metaphor*.

DAVIES, C. 1989. "Goffman's concept of the total institution: Criticisms and revisions", *Human Studies*, Vol. 12, Nos. 1–2 (June), pp. 77–95.

DAVIS, M. 1975. Review of *Frame Analysis, Contemporary Sociology*, Vol. 4, No. 6 (November), pp. 599–603.

DELANEY, W. P. 1977. "The uses of the total institution: A Buddhist monastic example" in R. Gordon and B. Williams (eds), *Exploring Total Institutions*, Champaign, Il.: Stipes.

DE MAN, P. 1979. "The Epistemology of Metaphor" in S. Sacks (ed.), *On Metaphor*.

DENZIN, N. 1970. "Rules of Conduct and the Study of Deviant Behavior: Some Notes on the Social Relationship" in J. D. Douglas (ed.), *Deviance and Respectability*, New York: Basic Books.

—— and KELLER, C. 1981. "*Frame Analysis* reconsidered", *Contemporary Sociology*, Vol. 10, pp. 52–60.

DERRIDA, J. 1978a. *Writing and Difference*, London: Routledge and Kegan Paul.

—— 1978b. "The Retrait of Metaphor", *Enclitic*, Vol. 2, pp. 5–33.

—— 1982. *Margins of Philosophy*, Brighton, Sussex: Harvester.

—— 1987. *The Post Card. From Socrates to Freud and Beyond*, Chicago: University of Chicago Press.

DITTON, J. (ed.), 1980. *The View from Goffman*, London and Basingstoke: Macmillan.

DREW, P., and WOOTTON, A. (eds) 1988. *Erving Goffman: Exploring the Interaction Order*, Cambridge: Polity.

DURKHEIM, E. 1965. *The Elementary Forms of the Religious Life*, New York: The Free Press.

—— 1982. *The Rules of Sociological Method*, Basingstoke: Macmillan.

EMMISON, M. 1989. "A Conversation on Trial?", *Journal of Pragmatics*, Vol. 13, pp. 363–83.

ESTROFF, S. 1981. *Making it Crazy*. California: University of California Press.

EVANS, R. 1982. *The Fabrication of Virtue: English Prison Architecture, 1750–1840*, Cambridge: Cambridge University Press.

FOUCAULT, M. 1965. *Madness and Civilization*, New York: Vintage.

—— 1978. *Discipline and Punish*, London: Allen Lane.

GARFINKEL, H. 1967. *Studies in Ethnomethodology*, Englewood Cliffs (re-issued Cambridge: Polity, 1984).

—— 1974. "On Ethnomethodology" in R. Turner (ed.), *Ethnomethodology*.

GEERTZ, C. 1973. *The Interpretation of Cultures*, New York: Basic Books.

—— 1983. *Local Knowledge*, New York: Basic Books.

GIDDENS, A. 1984. *The Constitution of Society*, Cambridge: Polity.

—— 1987. *Sociology and Modern Social Theory*, Cambridge: Polity.

—— 1989. "A Reply to my Critics" in D. Held and J. Thompson, *Social Theory of Modern Societies*. Cambridge: Cambridge University Press.

—— 1990. *The Consequences of Modernity*, Cambridge: Polity.

GRIMSHAW, A. 1983. "Erving Goffman: A Personal Appreciation", *Language in Society*, Vol. 12, No. 1, pp. 147–8.

HABENSTEIN, R. 1954. "The American Funeral Director" (unpublished Ph.D. dissertation), University of Chicago.

*Harvard Guide to Influential Books*. See Maury Devine and Dissel.

HERITAGE, J. 1984. *Garfinkel and Ethnomethodology*. Cambridge: Polity.

IGNATIEFF, M. 1978. *A Just Measure of Pain*, London and Basingstoke: Macmillan.

—— 1983. "Life at Degree Zero", *New Society* (20 January).

JACKALL, R. 1988. *Moral Mazes*, Oxford: Oxford University Press.

JAMESON, F. 1976. "Review of *Frame Analysis*", *Theory and Society*, Vol. 13, pp. 119–33.

JEFFERSON, G. 1984. "On the organization of laughter in talk about troubles" in J. Atkinson and J. Heritage, *Structures of Social Action*.

KENDON, A. (ed.) 1981. *Nonverbal Communication, Interaction and Gesture*, New York: Mouton Publishers.

LAKOFF, G., and JOHNSON, M. 1980. *Metaphors We Live By*, Chicago: Chicago University Press.

MACINTYRE, A. 1969. "The Self as Work of Art", *New Statesman* (28 March).

—— 1981. *After Virtue*, Brighton: Duckworth.

MARX, G. 1984. "Role Models and Role Distance: A Remembrance of Erving Goffman", *Theory and Society*, Vol. 13, No. 5, pp. 649–62.

—— 1989. *Undercover: Police Surveillance in America*, Twentieth Century Fund, California: University of California Press.

MANNING, P. 1989. "Resemblances", *History of the Human Sciences*, Vol. 2, No. 2, pp. 207–33.

—— 1989. "Ritual Talk", *Sociology*, Vol. 19, No. 3, pp. 365–85 (August).

—— 1991. "Goffman's Changing Use of the Dramaturgical Metaphor", *Sociological Theory* (Jan.–Feb.).

MAURY DEVINE, C., and DISSEL, C. M. (eds), *The Harvard Guide to Influential Books*, New York: Harper and Row.

MAYNARD, D. 1984. *Inside Plea Bargaining*, New York: Plenum.

—— and ZIMMERMAN, D. 1984. "Topical Talk, Ritual and the Social Organization of Relationships", *Social Psychology Quarterly*, Vol. 47, No. 4, pp. 301–16.

MESSINGER S., SAMPSON, H., and TOWNE, R. 1962. "Life as Theater: Some Notes on the Dramaturgic Approach to Social Reality", *Sociometry*, Vol. 14, No. 2 (July), pp. 141–63.

MILLER, T. 1984. "Goffman, Social Acting and Moral Behavior", *Journal for the Theory of Social Behavior*, Vol. 14, No. 2, pp. 141–63.

—— 1987. "Goffman, Positivism and the Self", *Philosophy of the Social Sciences*, Vol. 16, pp. 177–95.

MOUZELIS, N. 1971. "On Total Institutions", *Sociology*, Vol. 5, No. 1, pp. 113–20.

NEHAMAS, A. 1985. *Nietzsche: Literature as Life*, Cambridge, Mass.: Harvard University Press.

NIETZSCHE, F. 1968. *The Will to Power* (Trans. W. Kaufmann), New York: Vintage Books.

PERRY, N. 1974. "The Two Cultures and the Total Institution", *British Journal of Sociology*, Vol. 25, pp. 245–55.

QUINE, W. 1979. "A Postscript on Metaphor" in S. Sacks. (ed.), *On Metaphor*.

RAWLS, A. 1989. "Language, self and social order: A reformulation of Goffman and Sacks, *Human Studies*, Vol. 12, Nos, 1–2 (June), pp. 147–72.

RICHARDS, I. 1965. *The Philosophy of Rhetoric*, Oxford: Oxford University Press.

RICOEUR, P. 1986. *The Rule of Metaphor*, London: Routledge and Kegan Paul.

RORTY, R. 1986. "The Contingency of Community", *London Review of Books*, (July).

ROSENHAN, D. 1973. "On Being Sane in Insane Places", *Science*, pp. 250–8.

ROTHMAN, D. 1971. *The Discovery of the Asylum*, Boston: Little, Brown and Co.

RYAN, A. 1978. "Maximising, minimising, moralising" in C. Hookway and P. Petitt (eds), *Action and Interpretation*, Cambridge: Cambridge University Press.

SACKS, H., SCHEGLOFF, E., and JEFFERSON, G. 1974. "A Simplest Systematics for the Organization of Turn-Taking for Conversation, *Language*, Vol. 4, pp. 696–735.

SACKS, S. (ed.) 1979. *On Metaphor*, Chicago: University of Chicago Press.

SCHEGLOFF, E. 1982. "Discourse as an interactional achievement: some uses of 'uh huh' and other things that come between sentences" in A. Scull, *Decarceration*.

—— 1988. "Goffman and the Analysis of Conversation" in P. Drew and A. Wootton (eds), *Erving Goffman: Exploring the Interaction Order*, Cambridge: Polity.

—— and SACKS, H. 1974. "Opening Up Closings" in R. Turner (ed.), *Ethnomethodology*. Harmondsworth: Penguin.

SCHELLING, T. 1960. *The Strategy of Conflict*, Cambridge, Mass.: Harvard University Press.

SCULL, A. 1984. *Decarceration: Community and the Deviant – A Radical View* (2nd edn), Cambridge: Polity.

SEARLE, J. 1969. *Speech Acts*, Cambridge: Cambridge University Press.

SEDGWICK, P. 1982. *Psycho Politics*, London: Pluto Press.

SENNETT, R. 1977. *The Fall of Public Man*, Cambridge: Cambridge University Press.

SHARROCK, W. 1976. "Review of Frame Analysis", *Sociology*, Vol. 10, pp. 332–4.

SIMMEL, G. 1950. *The Sociology of Georg Simmel* (ed. K. Wolff), New York: Free Press.

—— 1978. *The Philosophy of Money* (trans. T. Bottomore), London: Routledge, Kegan and Paul.

—— 1989. "A Simmelian Reading of Goffman" (unpublished dissertation), University of Salford, England.

SOSKICE, J. 1985. *Metaphor and Religious Language*, Oxford: Clarendon Press.

SWANSON, G. 1975. Review of *Frame Analysis* in *Annals of the American Academy of Political and Social Science*, Vol. 420 (July), pp. 218–20.

SZASZ, T. 1990. *The Untamed Tongue*, La Salle, Il.: Open Court.

TANNEN, D. (ed.), *Georgetown University Roundtable on Languages and Linguistics* (pp. 71–93). Washington, DC: Georgetown University Press.

TAXEL, H. 1953. "Authority Structure in a Mental Hospital Ward" (unpublished Master's thesis), Department of Sociology, University of Chicago.

TURNER, R. (ed.) 1974. *Ethnomethodology*, Middlesex: Penguin.

VERHOEVEN, J. 1985. "Goffman's frame analysis and modern micro-sociological paradigms in Helle H. and Eisenstadt S. (eds), *Micro Sociological Theory*, New York: Sage.

WATSON, R. 1987. "Reading Goffman on Interaction" (unpublished Paper).

WEBER, M. 1949. *The Methodology of the Social Sciences*, New York: The Free Press.

WHYTE, W. H. 1988. *City*, New York: Basic Books.

WIEDER, L. 1974. "Telling the Code" in R. Turner (ed.), *Ethnomethodology*.

WILLIAMS, R. 1980. "Goffman's Sociology of Talk" in J. Ditton (ed.), *The View from Goffman*.

—— 1983. "Sociological Tropes: A Tribute to Erving Goffman", *Theory, Culture and Society*, Vol. 2, No. 1.

—— 1988. "Understanding Goffman's Methods" in P. Drew and

A. Wootton, *Erving Goffman: Exploring the Interaction Order*.

WILLOUGHBY, R. H. 1953. "The Attendant in the State Mental Hospital" (unpublished Master's thesis), Department of Sociology, University of Chicago.

WINKIN, Y. 1988. Erving Goffman: *Les Moments et leurs hommes*, Paris: Minuit.

WITTGENSTEIN, L. 1972. *Philosophical Investigations*, Oxford: Basil Blackwell (first published 1953, 2nd edn 1958).

# Index

Note: Titles of Goffman's works are in **bold**.